"All That Glitters":
Prospecting for Information in the Changing Library World

FOUNDATIONS IN LIBRARY AND INFORMATION SCIENCE, Volume 44

Editors: Thomas W. Leonhardt, *Director of the Library, Oregon Institute of Technology*

Murray S. Martin, *University Librarian and Professor of Library Science Emeritus, Tufts University*

"All That Glitters":
Prospecting for Information in the Changing Library World

Edited by STEVEN VINCENT
SOUTHERN POLYTECHNIC
STATE UNIVERSITY
and SUE K. NORMAN
DICKINSON COLLEGE

JAI PRESS INC.
Stamford, Connecticut

Library of Congress Cataloging-in-Publication Data

All that glitters : prospecting for information in the changing library world / edited by Steven Vincent and Sue K. Norman.
        p.   cm. — (Foundations in library and information science ; v. 44)
Includes bibliographical references and index.
ISBN 0-7623-0602-5
  1. Information resources—Evaluation—Study and teaching (Higher)—United States. 2. Computer network resources—Evaluation—Study and teaching (Higher)—United States. 3. Web sites—Evaluation—Study and teaching (Higher)—United States. I. Vincent, Steven. II. Norman, Sue K. III. Series.
ZA3060.A44   1999
025.04'071'173—dc21   99-047314
                                                          CIP

Copyright © 1999 JAI PRESS INC.
100 Prospect Street
Stamford, Connecticut 06901 1640

All rights reserved. No part of this publication may be reproduced, stored on a retrieval system, or transmitted in any form or by any means, electronic, mechanical, photocopying, filming, recording, or otherwise, without prior permission in writing from the publisher.

ISBN: 0-7623-0602-5

Library of Congress Catalog Number: 99-0-7314

Manufactured in the United States of America

CONTENTS

LIST OF ILLUSTRATIONS   vii

INTRODUCTION: THE SIREN'S SONG
   Steven Vincent and Sue K. Norman   ix

PANNING FOR GOLD IN THE CYBERSTREAM:
THE CURRENT STATE OF THE WWW AND THE
NEED FOR TEACHING EVALUTION SKILLS
   Douglas Cook   3

OBSTACLES TO TEACHING NOVICE
RESEARCHERS HOW TO EVALUATE THE
QUALITY OF WORLD WIDE WEB RESOURCES
   Steve Black   17

EVALUATION WORKOUT: EXERCISES AND
TECHNIQUES TO TEACH CRITICAL THINKING
ABOUT WEB RESOURCES
   Carol Doyle and Janet Martorana   35

A WEB PAGE IS NOT A PAGE: EVALUATING
DIGITAL INFORMATION
   Hal Kirkwood and D. Scott Brandt   55

EVALUATING WWW INFORMATION:
INSTRUCTION METHODS IN THE ELECTRONIC
CLASSROOM
   Jennifer Dorner and Susan Taylor   73

A RENAISSANCE IN EVALUTION SKILLS:
TEACHING STUDENTS TO EVALUATE
INFORMATION RESOURCES IN A GENERAL
EDUCATION PROGRAM
   Trudi E. Jacobson   91

TEACH THEM TO FISH IN A DIGITIZED AND
NON-DIGITIZED ENVIRONMENT:
DEMYSTIFYING PRINT SOURCES TO CREATE A
BALANCE BETWEEN THE ELECTRONIC AND
TRADITIONAL ENVIRONMENTS
    Bennie P. Robinson   103

USING TABLOID LITERATURE TO TEACH
CRITICAL READING SKILLS IN THE
INTERNET ERA
    Dan Ream   117

TEACHING WEB EVALUATION: MEETING THE
CHALLENGE
    Marsha Ann Tate and Jan Alexander   127

EXERCISES

NAME THAT COUNTRY! A MAP EXERCISE AS AN
INTRODUCTION TO THE LIBRARY REFERENCE
COLLECTION
    Izabella Tomljanovich   139

SIFTING DOWN TO THE GOLD: TEACHING
STUDENTS TO CRITICALLY EXAMINE WEB
SITES
    Julie Bockenstedt   143

TZMHR2: THE ANDERER EYE TEST
    Natasha Cooper   147

PANNING FOR GOLD: EVALUATION THROUGH
PROCESS RESEARCH APPROACH
    Sheryl Nisly-Nagele and Soo Lee   157

LIFE AND DEATH MATTER: INFORMATION
EVALUATION FOR NURSING IN THE REAL
WORLD
    Sandra Jamison and Soo Lee   167

ABOUT THE EDITORS   175

ABOUT THE AUTHORS   177

INDEX   183

LIST OF ILLUSTRATIONS

All cartoons were drawn by Kappa Waugh.

Just try http://www.directions/~penelope.com	1
Oh, Boy! Three thousand hits!	15
"Serbianrevenge.com may contain a touch of bias"	33
The URL ending with /I.Kant.getno.com	53
A great web site, but the URL had, you know, a tilde?	71
OK. Critical Thinking.	89
Who is the author of the site?	101
And I will show you indexes and abstracts beyond your dreams	115
Is the information current?	125

INTRODUCTION:
THE SIREN'S SONG

Steven Vincent and Sue K. Norman

The impetus for this book on evaluation in the library context springs from a poster session presented at the 1997 American Library Association Conference in San Francisco. Entitled, "Siren Song: The Lure of Technology and the Betrayal of Reality," the poster session focussed on teaching the need to evaluate information found on the Internet. It attracted a fair amount of attention at the conference, including several requests for articles on the subject from library journals. Since the presenters were neither the first nor the foremost to explore this area, the offer from JAI Press to edit a book seemed the most appealing offer, since it afforded us the opportunity to call upon several of the pioneers in Web source evaluation. The result is this collection of contributions from individuals who present their best thinking on the subject.

We also intended that the book should have a more practical side, much like a poster session. Therefore, the end of this volume contains exercises used by librarians in teaching Web evaluation in various settings.

THE FIVE LAWS

The framework for our poster session, and therefore this book, was an article by Michael Gorman in which he updated the five traditional laws of library service (1995). We believe that these new laws are particularly relevant to new technologies appearing in libraries.

The first of the new laws is "Libraries Serve Humanity." In library reference work, to serve is to answer the library user's question; but to do so effectively, it is necessary to find out what the real, often unasked question is. The questions we field are often couched in terms of technology ("How do I get on the Internet?") but the need is still for appropriate information. "Serving humanity" does not necessarily mean fulfilling individual cravings. We also have a duty to instruct, to direct library users to appropriate sources of information, and to get them to look beyond the often beguiling face of new technologies, such as the Web.

Gorman's Second Law is "Respect All Forms by Which Knowledge is Communicated." We should not be too hasty to discard older formats and embrace the new. Electronic formats are preferred for multimedia approaches, integrating text, images, and sound. They are also effective for rapid delivery of brief information. Print, however, is best for long-term storage of in-depth and detailed information. Electronic archives of book-length text may be a long way off, with notable exceptions such as Project Gutenberg. Storage and access requirements of many electronic databases also necessitate archiving older records in non-electronic formats, like microfilm or print. Many database providers keep only a certain number of years accessible in electronic format. Printed material is still preferred for reading, also. Web terminals in our libraries have actually increased the consumption of paper.

The third law is "Use Technology Intelligently to Enhance Service." As stated above, electronic formats are most effective for rapid delivery of current and brief information. However, electronic formats make it more difficult to evaluate information sources, since many of the traditional evaluation criteria (author, publisher, date, and coverage) are either absent or difficult to spot.

On the other hand, technology enhances the appeal of more traditional tools. Full-text databases and electronic indexing and abstracting tools are preferred over print sources of the same information. Electronic tools may even make traditional sources of information more widely available. In Georgia, for example, Project GALILEO makes electronic indexing available even in smaller libraries.

Gorman's Fourth Law tells us to "Protect Free Access to Knowledge." The Internet isn't free, even though it often appears to be. Many of the costs aren't apparent to the user, however. It always costs *something* to post information on the Internet, meaning that (a) some information is available only for a fee, and (b) some apparently free information is actually subsidized by advertising or interest groups, and therefore, slanted. Since the costs are hidden to the users, this means that they may not be aware of the slant.

Not everyone can afford the technology required to retrieve information from the Web. Not everyone owns a computer or has an Internet account. Libraries aim to make information freely available to all. Those who would publish on the Web face the same dilemma: although Web publishing is less expensive than traditional printing, not everyone has access to the technology or the skill base to make use of this medium. Also, since there is no traditional publishing apparatus or indexes to the Web, worthwhile information published on the Internet may not be received by the audience for whom it is intended.

Gorman's final law is "Honor the Past and Create the Future." This suggests that traditional and electronic formats need to complement each other. Our print-based libraries will not disappear in the near future, although there is a danger that policymakers may not recognize this and jeopardize the support for libraries. Libraries need to integrate newer technologies to promote the timely delivery of information.

According to Gorman's new laws, "Each new means of communication enhances and supplements all previous means" (1995, p. 784) Although the popular view is that each significant technological advance initiates a revolution that sweeps away obsolete technologies, the truth is that older technologies are never superseded in a single stroke. Technological revolutions may take decades, even centuries, before the superseded technologies are finally replaced. The history of an earlier information revolution illustrates this point: although parchment was introduced into Europe in the third century, it was not immediately accepted as the writing material of choice, and papyrus was still occasionally used as late as the twelfth century (Papyrus).

Is it possible that we are about to replace printed text on paper with electronic media? The answer is surely no, but a popular view prevails, even among a number of scholars, that we will see the death of the traditional book and library within a few years. In fact, the demise of the library has been predicted since the introduction of microform 70 years ago.

We need to recognize that each form of communication has different strengths which it brings to the task of disseminating or preserving knowledge. Among the strengths of print is its permanency—at least in comparison with the transient nature of the Web—as a storage medium. Print is also a better medium for accumulated knowledge, such as is found in books and encyclopedias. Since sustained reading at a computer terminal is uncomfortable at best, causing eye-strain and physical distress, paper is also a superior means of transmitting large amounts of information. When something useful is found in an online service, the Internet, or a CD-ROM, usually the first action is to print it for later reading under better conditions.

In contrast, the Internet expands the kind and amount of information accessible to the library user. Some kinds of information found on the Internet, such as online catalogs with product descriptions, are not usually found in libraries. The Internet also excels in the delivery of non-textual information. Images and sound are easily transmitted via the Internet and viewed or played from within a Web browser. The development of cross-platform multimedia standards, such as QuickTime, has even made it possible to deliver animation and sound over the Internet, something impossible to do with paper.

Although paper is an excellent means of reproducing color graphics, its publication is usually time-consuming and expensive. Internet images are delivered instantly, usually at no apparent cost to the user. Since the Internet is a fairly low-cost publishing medium, it is possible for individuals, not-for-profit organizations, and small businesses to become publishers. Many government agencies which are required to make the information they gather available to the public find the Internet an inexpensive way to meet their obligations. The down side of this is that while the Internet is a low-cost publishing medium, for many libraries the cost of the hardware, software, and computer expertise needed to provide access to this cheaply-published information remains a major expense. The government agencies have met their obligation to provide the information on the technical level only.

Since it is so inexpensive to publish on the Web, and it is so easy to update information, the Internet is ideal for delivery of timely information which changes frequently. The latest sports scores, stock prices, news headlines, and weather are the type of information well suited for the Web. However, although statistics and current awareness items are ideal for this venue, critical analyses of the content of Web-based information appear only in more traditional publishing formats, most often in printed scholarly journals.

Another attractive feature of the Internet is that it is already in electronic format. This makes it easy to download the information and massage it with a word processor. It also means that the indexing, searching, and retrieval of electronic information is superior to printed counterparts. Many libraries with access to electronic periodical indexing are canceling subscriptions to print equivalents. Others, however, are waiting to see how this volatile issue will sort out, and, if the electronic versions of these journals will contain *everything* the print version does. There have been many comparisons of the content of print and electronic versions of journals, and in these comparisons, the electronic version often comes up lacking. Letters to the editor are one example. Although these letters may not seem like major deletions, they are essential when documenting the conversations between scholars. If many libraries fail to hold the print issues, the conversations will be harder to follow, and many inexperienced researchers may not even realize that they are taking place.

THE REVOLUTION IN LIBRARY INSTRUCTION

Change has become a constant in the library world, but is it actually true that the more things change, the more they stay the same? Helping students perform their research efficiently and effectively has always been a priority with librarians, and the information revolution has given this assistance new importance, especially considering the manner in which students and faculty alike are using the new resources available to them.

Sir William Osler, 1849-1919, describes four types of readers in his *Aphorisms* (1950):

> An old writer says that there are four sorts of readers: Sponges, which attract all without distinguishing; Howre-glasses, which receive and powre out as fast; Bagges, which retain the degrees of the spices and let the wine escape; and SIEVES, which retain the best only. A man wastes a great many years before he reaches the "sieve" stage.

Librarians and faculty are becoming aware that with the seemingly endless supply of information available to campuses, particularly through the Internet and World Wide Web, the students are behaving like sponges, eagerly absorbing anything with which they come in contact.

Although the need to help students evaluate the information found during the research process has grown more critical, the evaluation process is often slighted—if not totally ignored—in an instruction session. Faculty assume that students assess their research automatically, but don't realize that evaluation is an acquired skill. Therefore, librarians need to place increased stress on evaluation methods and skills, placing it at the top of their instruction agenda by giving it primary emphasis in an instruction session, rather than a brief mention at the end or skipping it altogether.

Several authors have noted that students are generally uncritical about information they find with the computer. Martorana and Doyle (1996, p. 186) call this "the seduction factor": students prefer to use the computer whether or not more relevant print resources are available and they seldom question the results of their search or their search strategy. Oberman (1991, p. 108) believes that online resources tend to give students a false sense of confidence in their ability to use them effectively. The result too often is that students, assigned to find scholarly articles, use a Yahoo! or Hotbot to find Web pages. They may not fully understand how to use the search engine they select, rarely recognize that scholarly articles are almost never found on Web pages, and never question what they find.

Oberman (1991, p. 113) suggests that since students see the computer as having all the answers, they see no need to understand the relationship between their information needs and the online resources at their disposal. They view the computer as the sole source of information and haven't developed the cognitive skills to select an appropriate database or Internet search tool to assure that they will find the information they require. Unfortunately, many faculty also have the same perception of the online environment. How often do students come to the library with an assignment to find an article on an overly broad topic such as "databases," or "to use the computer to find three articles"?

As Martorana and Doyle (1996, p. 185*ff*) point out, the computer itself creates obstacles to teaching critical thinking skills. In addition to the "seduction factor," they identify two other factors which impede the learning process. "Noise distraction" is caused by students' varying degrees of comfort with the computer. Those with limited computer exposure are intimidated by the hardware, while those with more expertise wander off in their own directions. The "confusion factor" is essentially the same condition identified by Oberman (1991, p. 107) as the "cereal syndrome": students are overwhelmed by the number of choices available. When faced with a bewildering selection of information resources, most fall back on one or two with which they have become comfortable, rather than attempt to find the one best suited to their information need.

For good or ill, therefore, the library is drawing closer to the computer lab. Rabinowitz (1997, p. 19) has noted that students too often assume that all relevant information on a topic may be found on the Internet. More alarmingly, many faculty appear to share this misconception. Combined with the library's increasing reliance on online catalogs, CD-ROM's, and other electronic resources, many faculty expect library instruction to focus on tool use, rather than on critical thinking and evaluating information. As Oberman (1991, p. 114) suggests, although the cognitive skills needed to perform research effectively have remained essentially the same, our teaching methods must change.

The traditional "show and tell" presentation in which librarians brought samples of print resources for the students to see is no longer a valid form of instruction. Since the ease of Web access can cause faculty and student alike to think that they don't require instruction, the librarian must find more dynamic ways to alert their constituents to the new resources available, how to use them, and most importantly, how to evaluate what they find when they use them. Hands-on instruction in computer-equipped library classrooms has almost become a necessity today. Since students gravitate to the Web, using the Web itself for instruction catches the student's interest at the outset. Many libraries now maintain Web pages with evaluation tips and exercises or lists of recommended Internet resources. (URL's for some sites and examples of exercises librarians have used in classes and in collaboration with faculty to teach evaluation skills are listed in the exercises at the end of the book.)

What is needed in classes is to stress access to information, rather than tool use. Rather than teaching how to use the computer to find information, instruction sessions need to emphasize two points: the need to evaluate information, wherever found, and how to pick a research tool appropriate to the information needed. Some areas in which students need guidance are whether to use print or online sources, whether they need to consult a periodical index or search the Web, how to choose an appropriate online database, and when searching the Internet, how to select an appropriate search tool.

Further, students need to be made aware that the research process is not an isolated sequence of steps—collecting information, reading, then writing a paper—but a cyclical process. Stating a question, gathering information, reading, and evaluating cannot be carried out independently of each other and may be repeated several times during the course of a research project. Evaluation may force a reexamination of the research question, necessitating further information gathering.

USE TECHNOLOGY INTELLIGENTLY

Gorman's Third Law directs us to "use technology intelligently to enhance service." (1995, p. 785) This means integrating new technologies into existing programs and services, and using them to seek solutions to problems. Although librarians have always been eager to embrace new technologies, whether parchment or PC, we have at times been too eager, seeking not answers, but applications of new technology. Each form of communication has an appropriate use, excelling either at preserving, retrieving, or disseminating information. This is what instruction sessions ought to focus on.

One example of the type of new instructional technology needed is employed by Martorana and Doyle (1996) in their classes at the University of California, Santa Barbara. They find that team teaching, assigning group tasks, and working with a variety of media successfully combat distraction, confusion, and seduction in an online classroom. Having an additional instructor in the classroom allows them to monitor student activities more closely, keeping those prone to wander on track, to provide more individualized instruction to those who need it, and to mix teaching and presentation styles, better holding the attention of the students. Group assignments allow students to pool their expertise and explore divergent paths, while bridging the gap between novice and experienced computer users. Using a variety of media holds students' interest and appeals to a variety of learning styles.

Martorana and Doyle introduce critical thinking skills by using a process-oriented approach, called "tool analysis," in which students learn to examine research tools critically. By learning to identify the scope of a research tool, including the subjects, time periods, geographical locations, or populations it covers, students are taught to determine if it is appropriate to their research need. By studying records from the tool, students learn to identify access points and the most effective way of searching it.

REFERENCES

Gorman, Michael. 1995. "Five New Laws of Librarianship." *American Libraries*: 784-785.
Martorana, Janet, and Carol D. Doyle. 1996. "Computers On, Critical Thinking Off: Challenges of Teaching in the Electronic Environment." *Research Strategies* 14:184-91.
Oberman, Cerise. 1991. "Avoiding the Cereal Syndrome, or Critical Thinking in the Electronic Environment." In *Information for a New Age: Redefining the Librarian*. Englewood, CO: Libraries Unlimited, 1995. Originally published in *Library Trends* 39 (3):189-202.
Osler, William, Robert Bennett Bean, and William Bennett Bean. 1950. *Aphorisms*. New York: H. Schuman.
Papyrus. In Britannica Online: http://www.eb.com/:80/cgi-bin/g?DocF=micro/451/4.html.
Rabinowitz, Celia. 1997. "Gathering Information: How to Get There from Here." *CRL News* 58 (1):19-20.

PANNING FOR GOLD IN THE CYBERSTREAM:
THE CURRENT STATE OF THE WWW AND THE NEED FOR TEACHING EVALUATION SKILLS

Douglas Cook

ABSTRACT

By describing the WWW metaphorically, a case is made for the need for teaching evaluation skills to students. Some of the difficulties which students may encounter on the WWW are as follows. First, students have a tendency to grab the first thing they find, since the WWW is so readily accessible. Students can easily get confused and wander aimlessly on the WWW without actually being able to find what they need. Students can become easily overwhelmed because of the huge amounts of information available on most topics. Students can find opposing opinions on most subjects on the WWW. Finally, because libraries have digitized a number of "traditional" sources and have made them accessible via the WWW, students get confused and cannot discern library resources from other WWW resources.

INTRODUCTION

Not long ago I taught a research skills session to a group of freshmen who were enrolled in Oral Communications. I was charged with empowering them with the skills they would need to find information for an "Informative Speech of Six Minutes in Length on a Topic of Current Interest." The assignment required them to locate all of their resources on the WWW. (They didn't have to use the library even once!) At the beginning of the session, the professor, a persuasive gentleman with a honey-tongue, painted a picture of the next millennium where everyone would need computer skills to survive. All knowledge would be available in computer format. All the great books, paintings, and compositions would become digitized and easily available to anyone with the skills to pull them down from the WWW. He went on to say that Dr. Cook, our Reference Librarian, was here today to impart knowledge so valuable to them that their future careers depended upon it. Just as scholars of an earlier time learned to unlock the secrets of the universe with the ability to use a quill pen, even so (yea, verily he said unto them) they would need to learn Internet skills as well.

For me, this short session was an epiphany of sorts. Sitting there, I saw my future pass before me. I had just started to learn about the Internet. I was enjoying my new found Internet skills and thought the Internet was pretty cool (I grew up in the 1960s so I am officially allowed to use the word "cool"). But would the future careers of these freshmen depend upon their WWW skills? Was I really teaching the research skills of the new millennium? (I hadn't thought about that). I had thought that I was just going to show them some new tricks that I had learned for finding information. While pondering these things in my heart, I went on to teach the freshmen how to get onto the WWW and how to use basic search engines to find information for an "Informative Speech of Six Minutes on a Topic of Current Interest."

Since that fateful day, eons of time in computer years has passed. (Alas, it was but a few semesters ago in real time). And some of the prophecies put forth by that good professor are coming to pass. More and more of the great books, paintings and compositions are being digitized. More and more scholars are using the WWW for their research. (And can I say it in public?) More and more librarians are spending more time on the WWW than they do handling books. Indeed, I have become the "WWW Librarian of the Quick and Dirty." (If I can't find the information in fifteen minutes on the WWW then I am not doing my job!) Our library home pages are available to students from any computer attached by umbilical cord to the Internet anywhere in the world. If we had a student in Timbuktu, she could get to our resources. The gold rush is on! Verily, the World Wide Web has become a goldmine of resources. Nuggets as big as card catalogs lie waiting to be gathered on the field of the ethernet. Students can strike it rich by panning for gold in the cyberstreams of the Web. Untold treasures wait to be quarried behind their computer screens.

But, while the students are staking their claims to the WWW planning to strike it rich, someone may have salted the mine. (Hark! Is that a claim jumper on the horizon?) Looks can be deceiving, as my dear old Grammy used to say. World Wide Web gold may turn out to be fool's gold. The nuggets may be nefarious. The metal may be masquerade. The bullion may be bogus. The treasure may be trash. The gold fields may be fallow. The quarry may be quirky. The excavation may be elusive. The mine may be misleading. The deposit may be disreputable. The digs may be depleted.

In order for our students to hit the mother lode, it will be necessary for us to give them a grubstake and help them to obtain the proper mining tools. Students will need to be taught appropriate search strategies so they can shovel their way through the mountains of ore. They will need to polish their magnifying lenses so they can scrutinize the nuggets they find to ensure that they haven't picked up fool's gold by mistake. They will need to sharpen their picks so they can hack away through the gravel surrounding the ore. For reasons which I am about to reveal, novice prospectors often are fooled into accepting base metal, rather than 24-carat gold. Students need your help to recognize card sharks, claim jumpers, con men, desperadoes, grifters, horse thieves, mine salters, outlaws, pickpockets, rowdies and other denizens of the gold fields of Cyberspace. Our job as instructional librarians is to teach students that all that glitters is not gold.

THE WWW IS LIKE A BIG MAC—THICK, JUICY, AND UBIQUITOUS

Kids spend many of their waking hours (maybe their half-waking hours) in school where the computer is a part of the classroom curriculum. Our educational institutions have had a love affair with technology for years.

It was recently estimated that "technology spending in K-12 public schools ... [is] twice the amount spent on textbooks."[1] In the early part of this decade a huge push was made to put computers into classrooms. More recently, however, public effort has been spent on connecting those computers to the Internet. President Clinton's Technology Literacy Challenge calls for an effort to connect every public school classroom to the Internet by the year 2000. By the end of 1997, 78% of the public schools in the U.S. were connected to the Internet.[2] In school, students work with computers on a daily basis and many of those students now spend time on the WWW.

Such time is spent in an attractive environment. The WWW consists mainly of galvanizing graphics. The multimedia melange of the WWW provides an atmosphere of acute activity, sundry short sound bites and great gobs of information. Students can use the Web to chat with other virtual inhabitants of galactic Cyberspace. They can check out the latest movie reviews and sports scores, catch up on the doing of their soap opera heroines, stroll the courts of the cybermalls, and purchase anything their hearts desire (with Pop's credit card, of course). And, they can do all of this without changing out of their jammies!

Is it any wonder that your students would rather grab something from the WWW than get it from a book? (Students usually prefer a Big Mac to Mom's meatloaf, anyway, don't they?) We have a big job ahead of us, as library instructors. Rather than trying to do the impossible and woo the students back to the books, we need to make them savvy citizens of Cyberspace. Remember all of those lectures you've done about the difference between a "magazine" and a "journal" article? ("A journal article has a bibliography and a magazine article usually doesn't...") It's possible to apply the same type of logic to the evaluation of a document from the WWW. (Same song, different verse.) Don't throw out those old lecture notes. Dust them off and update them. Students should be taught that they need to find the best source of information for their needs no matter what the format.

THE WWW IS LIKE GRANDMA'S ATTIC—NOT VERY ORGANIZED BUT A FUN PLACE TO VISIT

Because of the way the WWW was created, no external structure has been imposed upon it. The WWW is comprised of about 30 million host computers all over the world linked together by communication lines.[3]

These computers are owned by businesses, agencies, organizations, universities and private citizens. Each computer has information stored in it which is accessible to anyone who is browsing the WWW. The information available on each computer is placed there by whomever owns the computer. There is no supervising agency which prescribes the content of any computer on the WWW. There are no Internet Collection Management Librarians to ensure that all topics are properly represented.

Because of this informal grass-roots growth structure, it is very hard to look at the WWW in an organized fashion. When I'm on the WWW, I occasionally have flashbacks of visiting my grandmother's attic when I was a kid. Decades worth of treasures were stored in boxes, chests and suitcases. Old clothing hung everywhere. Pieces of furniture, some still serviceable and some pretty useless, were piled in corners. Receipts and paraphernalia from the years Grammy ran a little neighborhood store were piled in dusty stacks. Albums of old pictures were stacked in corners. (They sure wore funny clothes in those days!) Cobwebby boxes of goodies that had belonged to my Dad when he was a kid—school papers, composition books, report cards—were everywhere. You get the idea. There was a lot of valuable stuff stored there and things with very little value at all, and some of it in total disorganization. It was a real chore for anyone to find something specific in that mess (although I certainly enjoyed rummaging through it). The WWW is like that—lots of stuff and little of it organized. Some of the things on the WWW are pretty valuable and some are pretty worthless. When you go looking for something on the WWW, you never know what you will find (but it sure is fun to browse).

Students need to be taught to bypass this total disorganization by learning organized search strategies. Particularly, search engines such as Yahoo[4] can help students in this task. Yahoo employs legions of educated persons to try to make sense of the wealth of sites on the WWW, by creating hierarchical lists of topics. (That sounds like a library, doesn't it?) Yahoo does not attempt to include everything on the WWW, but it tries to organize the "best" of the Web. Yahoo provides topical lists which can be searched or browsed. For students who have no idea where to start finding information on the WWW, Yahoo is the place to start.

If you look at Yahoo's main page you can see what I mean. Yahoo has fourteen main categories (Melville Dewey started with ten)—from

"Arts and Humanities" to "Society and Culture." It's possible to choose a topic and browse through the sub-topics until you find what you are looking for. For example, let's try to help one of the freshman I spoke to at the beginning of this treatise. He has chosen the "Death Penalty" for his "Informative Speech of Six Minutes in Length on a Topic of Current Interest." If you look at Yahoo's categories, one called "Society and Culture" stands out as the most likely to contain information about this topic. The "Society and Culture" page has a number of choices, including one for "Death." Next, the "Death" page includes, among other topics, "Capital Punishment." Finally, Yahoo's "Capital Punishment" page points out a number of links which will help explain both supporting and opposing viewpoints for the death penalty. There are also included a number of links to Web pages which have been created about specific persons who have been executed or who now reside on Death Row. As you can imagine, Yahoo is an excellent place to start research of this type. As long as students get to the right places on the WWW, they can often find answers to their questions. Learning to make their way through the mess is the problem.

USING THE WEB IS LIKE DRINKING FROM A FIRE HYDRANT—TOO MUCH, TOO FAST, AND SOMETIMES IT KNOCKS YOU ON YOUR BACK

There is an unbelievable amount of information on the WWW today. A peek at the statistics will boggle your mind. It is estimated that there will be 100 million users of the Internet this year.[5] During the summer of 1997 it was conjectured that there were 150 million documents available on the WWW.[6] Because of the gargantuan growth of the WWW, searching for anything is a chore, since it is not uncommon to get thousands of matches to a search. Recently I queried HotBot,[7] one of the most popular of the search engines. My search resulted in 8.5 million matches when I tried to find some information on the WWW about the word COMPUTER. Digging through 8.5 million documents can make your eyes glaze over.

This vast amount of information makes it imperative for students to learn the strategies of making the most of the search engines. Search engines do not have the ability to help differentiate between a match and a "match that really meets your needs." WWW search engines such as HotBot, randomly gather information from Web sites and create huge databases of words. The current search sites which claim to index the whole WWW (as does HotBot) use a type of computer program called a "spider" to visit WWW sites. These programs download whatever they find. This downloaded information is then indexed. This whole process is entirely computerized. No librarian ever checks to make certain the words are spelled correctly. No librarian checks to make certain that the words found at a Web site are actually representative of the majority of the information there. And, no librarian adds subject authorities to these databases. All this can be very confusing to the uninitiated.

Let me give you an example. Recently a student came to the Reference Desk saying that she had to do a paper on "computers in elementary education" and she had to use the WWW as her major resource. We went to HotBot and did a simple search for COMPUTERS ELEMENTARY EDUCATION (essentially a Boolean search with the words combined with the default AND). We got a hit list of over 71,000 matches ranked in "relevancy" order. (Basically, the more times a word is mentioned in a document or the closer it is mentioned to the beginning of the document, the more "relevancy" points the document gets and is, therefore, placed closer to the top of the list). So even though the most "relevant" matches are listed first, these choices have been made by a computer. The hit at the top of the chart, in this case, was a site called SuperQuest[8]–an educational site about science and technology for kids aged 8-14. Although this site is really more about science than it is about computers in elementary schools, because our three search terms were included on the first page of this Web site, the search engine thought it was a match.

We continued searching. My freshman and I used our reasoning skills to redefine our search a bit. This time we looked for ELEMENTARY EDUCATION as a phrase (COMPUTERS AND "ELEMENTARY EDUCATION"). We narrowed the field from 71,000 to a mere 5,000. This time the hit at the top of the chart was a page for North Country School,[9] a privately owned boarding school in the mountains of New York State which features computers in its elementary education program. After this, we had to dig down through several other pages of matches before we found anything which came close to meeting our needs. The first useful site we found was created by a graduate student at Temple University in Philadelphia.[10] It was called "Computers in Elementary Education" and had links to educational sites, lesson plans, and ideas for using computers in the K-8 curriculum. Even though this site was on our topic, we still needed to follow several links from this site to actually get any real information which could be used as fodder for a speech.

The moral of this story is that even though we used this particular search site to its maximum, we still had to use our brains just to pick a potential match from the list. There is too much information available on the WWW for the search engines to make sense of it. No search engine currently available has the ability to take the place of your brains and truly find a match for you.

THE WWW IS A SOAPBOX—ANYONE CAN SAY JUST ABOUT ANYTHING, AND THEY DO

The current state of politics in the United States is such that the WWW has become a platform for freedom of expression. Any idea you can think of—true or false; liberal or conservative, pornographic or politically correct; good, bad, or ugly—is represented on the WWW. There are no Internet Thought Police. (Big Brother isn't watching.) Anyone with access to the WWW can put whatever he or she desires on a Web page. (This is as it should be; after all, haven't libraries been bastions of the freedom of expression for ages?)

One of my favorite examples of this is a White House parody page. I like to use this when I want to show students that they can't believe everything they see on the WWW. President Clinton's actual home page address is : http://www.whitehouse.gov.[11] Our tax dollars at work have made this a very well-designed site. It has attractive graphics, and it's easy to search. It even has useful resources relating to the Executive Branch, including such valuable information as the President's daily press releases.

If you change the address a bit and type in http://www.whitehouse.net,[12] you get a parody of the White House page created by two crazy guys not connected with the federal government in any way—Bill Herrin and Chris Mincer. The graphics mimic the real thing almost exactly. You need to look pretty closely and think about what you are seeing to tell the difference. The subtle giveaway is a picture of Beavis and Butthead as our President and Vice-President. (Is there really a BMS? Bureau of Missing Socks?) I like to spring this on unsuspecting freshmen when we are talking about finding information on the WWW.

(You can probably tell by now that I was a teenage fan of *Mad Magazine*.) The address of this parody site really gives no clue to the novice that they are not at the real White House site. It is only by closely examining these pages that students realize that their legs are being pulled. (By the way, don't try http:// www.whitehouse.*com*[13] in class as I did several weeks ago when I jumbled the address. I got more of a reaction than I had planned for.)

Because students really can run across ideas of every sort on the WWW, it's absolutely vital that they learn to strengthen their innate powers of observation and deduction. One of the best WWW sources of information regarding evaluation is "Evaluating WWW Resources."[14] This Web page was put together by librarians Jan Alexander and Marsha Tate. They take five familiar criteria for evaluating traditional print resources and apply them to the evaluation of WWW resources. The criteria are accuracy, authority, objectivity, currency, and coverage. I like this approach, because I think that WWW resources should be evaluated in a similar fashion to print resources.

THE WWW IS LIKE A LIBRARY—OR IS THE LIBRARY LIKE THE WWW?

If all this wasn't confusing enough, the past year has seen a merging of the old standard reliable resources, such as CD-ROM databases and computerized card catalogs, with the WWW. It is not uncommon for students to be able to search the WWW, as well as standard library resources from the same WWW browser. Take a look at the "Electronic Resources" of your library's Web site. Students can find information on any topic. They can find the full-text of magazine articles. Students can look something up in an encyclopedia or read a newspaper. Many of these services which we provide from our home pages are not what I would call "WWW Resources." They are computerized databases accessed through the same Web browser as the information on the WWW. To the initial confusion of our students, we have made a virtually seamless interface between computerized standard resources and information on the WWW.

We should not be surprised when students have no idea what they are getting, nor from where they are getting it. Often when students come to the Reference Desk with questions about a resource they have pulled from a computer, they have no idea of the source of what they have printed. I wish I had a dime for every blank look that I've gotten at the Reference Desk when I've asked, "Where did you get this citation?" The typical answer is "From that computer over there." It used to be easier in the olden days. If you wanted a magazine article, you went to the *Reader's Guide to Periodical Literature*. If you wanted a newspaper article, you went to the *New York Times Index*. If you wanted a brief summary of a topic, you went to the *Encyclopedia Britannica*. If you wanted a book, you went to the card catalog. Students knew where they were and what they would find when they got there. (Didn't they?)

In this new world of virtual libraries, students need to be taught to identify their surroundings while they are doing their research. This isn't a new problem. Librarians have been telling students how to differentiate between types of resources for a long time. I think the crux of this matter is arousing the student's powers of observation. Students are too trusting of the resources they find; they need to become skeptics. They need to have the batteries in their thinking caps charged and to wear them all the time. (Maybe we should hand thinking caps out at the door?)

CONCLUSION

Will the future employability of our freshmen depend on their ability to search the World Wide Web? Maybe. Will the computer become the "quill pen" of the new millennium? Probably. Will humankind's entire store of knowledge become encoded into the computers that make up the Internet? Possibly. Will students ever need to darken the door of another library? I hope so, I will miss them if they don't. Will students need to use the same evaluation skills when searching the WWW that they always have used when searching traditional sources? Yes. Will the WWW remain as confusing for freshmen to search as libraries always have been strange places to the uninitiated? I think so. Will Jo Freshman find a topic for her "Informative Speech of Six Minutes in Length on a Topic of Current interest"? (Tune in tomorrow, Same time. Same channel.)

So, put on your hard hat. Load up your burro. Strap on your grub sack. Grab your pick and shovel. Get ready to join the gold rush. In your excitement to hit the trail, don't forget your teaching skills and your magnifying glass. Line up your students. Fire up your Web browser. We're off to the gold mines. (California or bust!)

NOTES

1. David A. Kaplan and Adam Rogers, "The Silicon Valley." *Newsweek* 127 (17)(April 22, 1996): 60-61. [ONLINE]. Available from IAC, Database: SearchBank Expanded Academic ASAP [accessed February 25, 1998]
2. John Bare and Anne Meek, *Internet Access in the Public Schools.* [ONLINE]. January 1998. Available from http://nces.ed.gov/pubsearch/pubsinfo.asp?pubid=98031X XXXX [accessed March 10, 1998].
3. Network Wizards, *Internet Domain Survey.* [ONLINE]. January 1998. Available from http://www.nw.com/zone/WWW/report.html [accessed March 10, 1998].
4. *Yahoo.* [ONLINE]. Available from http://www.yahoo.com [accessed March 10, 1998].
5. Mary Furlong and Stefan B. Lipson. "Trekking the Internet," *Saturday Evening Post* 269, no. 3 (May-June 1997): 54-58 [ONLINE]. Available from the IAC, Database: SearchBank Expanded Academic ASAP [accessed February 27, 1998].
6. Daniel Sullivan, *How Big Are the Search Engines?* [ONLINE]. Available from http://searchenginewatch.com/size.htm [accessed October 18, 1997].
7. *HotBot.* [ONLINE]. Available from http://hotbot.com [accessed March 10, 1998].
8. *SuperQuest.* [ONLINE]. Available from http://www.superquest.com [accessed March 10, 1998].
9. *North Country School.* [ONLINE]. Available from http://www.nct.org/school/school.htm [accessed March 19, 1998].
10. Jane Allison, *Computers in Elementary Education.* [ONLINE]. Available from http://nimbus.temple.edu/~jallis00 [accessed March 10, 1998].
11. *White House.* [ONLINE]. Available from http://www.whitehouse.gov [accessed March 10, 1998] *Note:* this is the genuine White House home page.
12. *White House.* [ONLINE]. Available from http://www.whitehouse.net [accessed March 10, 1998] *Note:* This is the amusing parody of the White House home page.
13. *White House.* [ONLINE]. Available from http://www.whitehouse.com [accessed March 10, 1998]. *Note.* This is the naughty page which uses the name White House.
14. Janet E. Alexander and Marsha A. Tate, *Evaluating Web Resources.* [ONLINE]. Available from http://www.science.widener.edu/~withers/webeval.htm [accessed March 2, 1998].

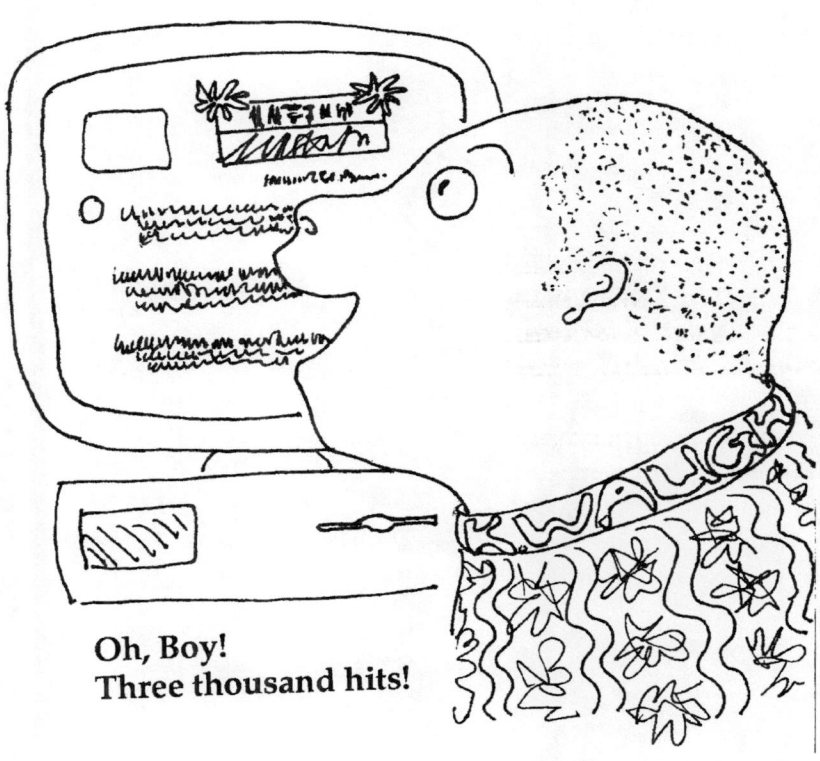

OBSTACLES TO TEACHING NOVICE RESEARCHERS HOW TO EVALUATE THE QUALITY OF WORLD WIDE WEB RESOURCES

Steve Black

ABSTRACT

Teachers' and librarians' efforts to teach students to evaluate information sources face significant obstacles. Learning to apply criteria to judge the quality of web resources is limited by students' background knowledge, teachers' overly optimistic assumptions about students' research abilities, the impossibility of defining a set of universally applicable criteria, the aesthetic and practical difficulties of defining quality, and the vast, uncontrolled nature of the web. Each of these obstacles is discussed, with an emphasis on the challenges to teaching novice researchers, particularly college freshmen. Suggested strategies for overcoming the obstacles are provided for teachers, librarians, and students.

Teaching the skills needed to evaluate the quality of information resources found on the World Wide Web remains of great interest in the late 1990s. The medium is still relatively new, the information on the

WWW is quantitatively and qualitatively different from traditional library collections, and student inabilities to effectively evaluate the quality of information resources are amplified when they use the web. The web has democratized the communication of ideas by giving information producers of all stripes an effective way to bypass traditional gatekeepers of information. Because of its uncontrolled content, teachers and librarians have a duty to teach students to evaluate the quality of information on the WWW. "Teachers" as discussed here will encompass instructors in both secondary and higher education, with a special emphasis on teachers of novice researchers in the bodies of college freshmen.

HURDLES IN THE WAY OF STUDENT LEARNING

Regardless of educational level, roadblocks stand in the way of teachers' and librarians' efforts to teach students to evaluate information sources. Learning to apply criteria for judging the quality of web resources is limited by students' background knowledge, teachers' overly optimistic assumptions about students' research abilities, the impossibility of defining a set of universally applicable criteria, the aesthetic and practical difficulties of defining quality, and the vast, uncontrolled nature of the web. Heightened awareness of the impediments to learning to evaluate the quality of WWW resources should help improve evaluation skill instruction.

Background Knowledge

Perhaps the most fundamental obstacle to learning to evaluate the quality of WWW resources is students' insufficient background knowledge to meaningfully apply criteria of judgement, regardless of the information medium. Even before the WWW, students often had insufficient knowledge to effectively judge the reliability, authority, and accuracy of information, especially in fields new to them. Students lacking the background knowledge to apply criteria of judgement to web resources have trouble evaluating print resources, too. But the universe of research information in the pre-web world was dominated by books and journals found in the library. Most of what students found in the library met nominal standards of quality, as determined by publishers, editors, peer reviewers, and librarians. The publishers' and librarians' gatekeeping function provided a safety net. A student could rather blindly navigate through the literature, and most anything they found would be acceptable for a research paper. Perhaps not appropriate for *their* paper, but at least intended to meet basic standards of credibility, authority, and accuracy. Academic library collections were and are ideally a preserve for the scholarly frame of reference.

Time

The range of scholarly accomplishment is vast, and the level to which students are expected to achieve varies. But at all levels, scholarship requires basic factual knowledge and familiarity with themes, methods, and important lines of inquiry. Students do not always readily buy into the scholarly frame of reference, and when they do, it can take more than a few semesters of encouragement for the message to sink in. Many students are not easily enculturated, and tend to resist accepting the work load that scholarship requires. The time that must be invested in approaching an issue in a scholarly fashion, including gaining sufficient background knowledge to meaningfully evaluate information, is far from trivial. A study by Carver (1982) suggests that the optimal reading rate for a balance of speed and comprehension for a typical college student is 300 words per minute. A widely accepted median reading rate for incipient freshmen (twelfth graders) is 250 words per minute (Harris & Sipay, 1985, p. 533). Thus a freshman reading at the median rate would have to devote about 22 minutes to this 5,400-word chapter, not counting time for interruptions and pauses to think about what is being read. Freshmen reading below the median would take significantly longer.

Novice researchers may not be aware of how much reading time they are expected to invest. Even when they are aware, reading loads an experienced researcher accepts as normal may appear prohibitive to a novice.

Perspective

The clash of frames of reference between professorial expectations and student performance extends beyond reading time and work load. The world view and critical thinking abilities of a novice researcher are dramatically different from the scholarly frame of reference professors acquire as they earn a doctoral degree, scramble to land an academic position, and struggle to achieve rank and tenure. Ph.D.'s internalize a broad array of critical thinking skills as they produce their original research, stay current in their fields, and publish.

The abilities to find and judge sources that have become second nature to a professor bewilder the typical freshman. Unrealistic faculty expectations and student bewilderment are the focus of "Desperately Seeking Citations" (Leckie, 1996). Writing from the perspective of a librarian, Leckie describes how instructors, who are trained as expert researchers and skilled in all it takes to produce original research, try to apply their model of research to novices. But the novices have none of the characteristics an expert researcher possesses. A student new to a field, exposed only to a textbook, reserve materials, and lectures, has no way of knowing who the important researchers are, what topics are considered important, or which journals have good reputations. While the professor wishes them to devise a good information-seeking strategy, students are usually just searching for a means to cope. Leckie describes common assumptions that lead professors to give research assignments that exceed most undergraduates' research abilities. The gist of the assumptions is that students will become familiar with the literature in a brief amount of time, and that they can navigate the literature on their own. As an experienced librarian, Leckie knows that most students, especially freshmen, will not or can not efficiently gain necessary background knowledge in a new field without considerable guidance and support.

The inappropriate use of WWW resources in student papers is a symptom of this clash of frames of reference, this gap between faculty expectations and student performance. Over-reliance on and misplaced faith in web resources stem both from students' desire to save time and their insufficient ability to judge the quality of sources. Students turn to the web in the often misplaced belief that it will save time over traditional research methods. The ability to put in a search string, link to some pages, hit Print or Download and Bingo! have the documents in hand is a powerful lure. In many cases, a student can find some web page on a topic more quickly than he or she could find a document using indexes and journals or books. In fact, in some cases, the web search approach works quite well. But information content on the WWW is very hit-or-miss, and the odds of finding a high quality document in any particular field are fairly long. (Licensed full-text databases available via WWW access may be exceptions. This discussion of WWW resources refers specifically to that which is available for "free").

Information Traps

Persistence is a virtue in research, but the wide gaps in quality information on the web make tenacity there risky business. Unfortunately, students who mistakenly believe that "everything is on the web" are likely to either waste an enormous amount of time, settle for any plausibly relevant document, or both. The harm in wasting time on fruitless WWW searches is that it crowds out time that should be spent looking for books, journal articles, or other reliable resources. The harm in settling for any plausible document is that the sources will likely fail to meet the standards of authority, accuracy, objectivity, currency, and coverage expected of any source cited in a research paper. Either way, the quality of sources will fall short of the teacher's expectations, and the quality of the research report will suffer. Teachers can ameliorate student misuse of the web by making expectations clear and specifying the standards of citable sources. Instruction in how to use search engines and to evaluate web resources can certainly help, and placing specific limits on the use of web resources for a particular project may be appropriate. The harder nut to crack is the problem of students having inadequate background knowledge to apply criteria of evaluation.

A simple exercise with a printed index can demonstrate the experience and knowledge required to judge resources. Take a group of printed citations on a topic of your choice, and name a research topic based on the index heading. For instance, choose the index heading Music Festivals—New York from *Reader's Guide to Periodical Literature* covering 1969, and the topic "cultural impact of Woodstock." Pick three citations that strike you as being relevant to the chosen topic, that are likely to have some intellectual substance, and that represent diverse viewpoints. Now recruit a novice researcher. Give the novice the page of citations and the topic, and ask them to pick the three best citations. Tell them that "best" means relevant, substantive, and diverse. Compare selections.

The odds are very good that the experienced researcher will make different, and apparently superior, selections from those of the novice. Several reasons exist for this, all based on experience. In the first place, the novice researcher may have an inadequate understanding of the concepts "relevant," "substantive," and "diverse." Beyond that, the novice may not recognize standard clues to quality. The experienced researcher knows to pick up clues from journal titles, the wording of article titles, and the lengths of articles, all based on familiarity gained from reading journals. The researcher will likely skip *Hi Fi* and *Seventeen*, and will know that the point of view in "Mass infantilism, anyone?" in the *National Review* will be different from "Ultimate Pop experience" in *Saturday Review*. The novice may have no familiarity with *National Review*, may not know the perspective of *Hi Fi*, may not realize why *Seventeen* should be passed over, may indeed not know the meaning of "infantilism." Recognizing these clues appears simple and obvious. But they are neither simple nor obvious to a novice researcher.

WHAT IS RELIABLE INFORMATION?

The problem of deficient background knowledge for judging information sources exists anywhere that frames of reference clash, even within professional scholarship. Take for instance the "*Social Text* Affair." In Spring 1996, the cultural studies journal *Social Text* published Alan Sokal's "Transgressing the Boundaries: Toward a Transformative Hermeneutics of Quantum Gravity" (Sokal, 1996a). Sokal wrote the article as a parody, but did not tell the editors it was meant as such. Three weeks after publication, Sokal revealed his hoax in *Lingua Franca* (Sokal, 1996b), and a heated public debate ensued. Judging the merits of Sokal's arguments vis-à-vis postmodernist critiques far exceeds my qualifications. My background knowledge of both physics and postmodernism is severely limited, and I am unwilling to devote the time to learn all that. But one aspect of the debate is directly relevant here. Sokal reports:

> [The *Social Text* Affair] proves only that the editors of *one* rather marginal journal were derelict in their intellectual duty, by publishing an article on quantum physics that they admit they could not understand, without bothering to get an opinion from anyone knowledgeable in quantum physics, solely because it came from a "conveniently credentialled ally" (as *Social Text* co-editor Bruce Robbins later candidly admitted), flattered the editors' ideological preconceptions, and attacked their "enemies" (Sokal, 1998).

In short, at least from Sokal's perspective, the editors failed, because of insufficient background knowledge and flawed judgement of the quality of a source, to keep the hoax outside the gates. Sokal's parody appeared in the supposedly reliable realm of peer-reviewed published research. So when students fail to judge quality by acceptable standards, they are not alone. Wherever frames of reference clash, unacceptable selections of information sources will occur, because what appears acceptable from one viewpoint can be unacceptable from another.

One must understand a viewpoint, including a healthy share of its knowledge base, to compare the merits of arguments or citations to arguments, or to "get" an article. Similarly, it takes a degree of knowledge to get a joke. For example, the staff of the *Annals of Improbable Research* annually honor people "whose achievements cannot or should not be reproduced" with Ig Nobel awards (Annals of Improbable Research, 1997). To find "Ig Nobel" funny, one needs to know three things: the purpose and prestige of Nobel prizes, the definition of ignoble, and the nature of the endeavors that win awards. One might not find "Ig Nobel" funny even knowing these three things, but without knowing them, one surely would not get the humor. The amount of knowledge required to "get" a scholarly paper is, of course, much greater than that which is required to "get" the spoof in a two-word title.

The 1997 Ig Nobel Prize for Meteorology went posthumously to Bernard Vonnegut for his paper in *Weatherwise*, "Chicken Plucking as Measure of Tornado Wind Speed" (Vonnegut, 1975). Vonnegut's one page article was obviously published with tongue firmly in cheek, but his paper follows an accepted format for a brief research article. References to serious works are properly cited, and the article follows the accepted format of reporting previous research, citing current research that informs a critique of the previous research, and drawing a conclusion about the applicability of the original research to present-day experimentation. The format, appearance and tone of the article are serious. The content, and really the content alone, contains the joke. The original research cited by Professor Vonnegut was the blasting of a chicken out of a six-pounder [cannon]. "The velocity was 341 miles per hour. A fowl, then, forced through the air with this velocity is torn entirely to pieces; with a less velocity, it is probable most of the feathers might be pulled out without mutilating the body." The research question that follows is whether loss of chickens' feathers can be a gauge of tornado wind speed. Vonnegut cites a number of scientifically demonstrated variables to conclude that "the plucking phenomenon is of doubtful value as an index [of tornado wind speed]". This strikes me as an absolutely hilarious gem of an article, and it apparently also so struck the bestowers of the Ig Nobel awards. But would everyone see the humor, and know the article was a jest?

A reader could apply generally accepted measures of the quality of a source, and rationally come to the conclusion that the article is reliable and accurate. And in a sense, it is. Every cited piece of research is presented seriously and correctly, even the original firing of a chicken from a cannon in 1842. Vonnegut concludes, after all, that the loss of chicken feathers is an unreliable indicator of tornado wind speed. Hopefully, a novice science student would recognize the fundamental absurdity of the research. But it is not certain that they would, especially if they uncritically applied a list of criteria for judging a source. And yes, a guide to critical thinking can be applied uncritically.

The point of this admittedly farcical example is that no set of criteria for judging the quality of a resource is universally applicable. Contexts change, as the meanings and intents of writers and readers change. Vonnegut's article is an example of seriously presenting an absurd point. Other writers, like Bernard's older brother Kurt, have presented absurdities to make serious points. No formula can address all the means by which valuable information is conveyed, because judging the quality of a resource requires sophisticated thinking grounded not only on knowledge of facts but also awareness of context. Lists of criteria are helpful, but inherently limited, because the art of determining accuracy and reliability has an essential subjective element. This is true regardless of the medium conveying the information being judged.

Hopefully, the aforementioned examples about Woodstock and chicken plucking would not apply to most college students, but as the *"Social Text* Affair" shows, the misjudgement of information quality occurs at more sophisticated levels. Judging quality requires not only knowledge and good judgement. To be done really well, it also requires an aesthetic sensibility; a sophisticated subjective sense of quality. Scholarly articles may be more often regarded for their utilitarian rather than their aesthetic qualities, but elegance, clarity, and creativity are still admired, and represent a desired standard for published research. Can this subjective sense be taught?

Who Defines Quality?

How do we know quality when we see it, and how can the ability to recognize quality be conveyed to students? A popular but thoughtful exploration of this issue can be found in Robert Pirsig's *Zen and the Art of Motorcycle Maintenance* (1974). Pirsig's creative journey in search of the meaning of quality travels into aesthetics and beyond. One path of inquiry relevant here incorporates a challenge to his composition students to answer the question, "What is quality in thought and statement?" (Pirsig, 1974, p. 184). His students have a very rough time with this abstract question. The students had been able to rank essays in order of quality, and seemed to have a degree of the subjective, aesthetic sense of quality. But they, and, at a different level, their teacher, find themselves unable to explain the root reasons behind the rankings. The teacher knows rhetoric's criteria of judgement, and how they are applied, but finds it effective to withhold conveying the criteria until after the students have struggled with the nature of quality as a subjective, but very real, thing. The teacher believes that it is pedagogically useful to leave quality undefined, because then students have to think for themselves, and judge for themselves. Only after their minds are thus engaged do the rhetorical criteria of unity, precision, depth, and so forth gain their full meaning. From Pirsig's point of view, then, lists of criteria may impede student understanding because it is better to have them grapple with the meaning of quality on their own.

As Pirsig notes along his journey, there remain persistent philosophical questions concerning the meaning of quality beyond questions of effective pedagogical methods. (Quality is meant here in an evaluative sense, rather than in the scientist's sense of describing characteristics). Prominent among these is whether quality is in the eyes of the beholder, or inherent in the thing itself. Is high quality objective, inherent in the object? Or is it subjective, existing only in the mind of the perceiver? If quality is objective, then a high quality scholarly article is consistently and universally of high quality. If quality is subjective, then an article is of high quality only in the context of the reader's understanding and intended use. Since it is quite impossible to solve this question here, let us skip to the assumption that the quality of scholarly publications is neither entirely subjective nor objective, but an amalgam of both perspectives. Unfortunately, printed and online guides to evaluating resources are forced to treat the resources as objects, and must assume that there are objective criteria that can be dispassionately applied to render a judgement of quality. But as the guides' creators know and express through statements about intended audience and author's purpose for publication, information quality only gains its full meaning in context. Objective criteria for measuring quality are necessary, but do not replace the need for subjective judgement. By their very nature, guides to evaluating information resources emphasize objective over subjective criteria, and need to be balanced with additional instruction in the art of assessment.

UNIQUE CHARACTERISTICS OF WWW RESOURCES

If the inherent subjectivity of evaluating quality and the necessity of background knowledge are old, what is new about evaluating the quality of WWW resources? Most obviously, evaluation of how effectively web sites use hypertext is a new application of aesthetic criteria. The hypertext linking; the marriage of text, sound, and visual images in web pages opens new potential for effectively conveying information. Just as cinema is judged by valid criteria that reach beyond the script, web sites may be properly judged by criteria beyond textual content. The quality of images and sounds, navigability, use of links, and even load time are relevant to the quality of a web site. In fact, guides for the evaluation of web resources are available that look almost exclusively at effective use of the medium as the standard of judgement, for instance "Web Evaluation for Secondary Grades" (Payton, 1997). While judging textual content and visual impact are not new, judging an information source by its effective use of links and its load time are newly specific to the web.

Also new by degree, if not by kind, is the impermanency of information on the web. Lost links and perpetual updates create problems requiring new application of evaluative skills. The flux of information on the web frustrates scholarship. With traditional resources, one did not have to ask, "Will this article still be in volume 20, issue 6, beginning on page 63 next year, and will the words be the same?" In the past, a published piece of information stayed in the same identifiable space, if it persisted anywhere at all, and the words remained as originally published. True, there are preservation issues with print, and things can be lost or vandalized. And grey literature presents special access problems. But if volume 20, issue 6, page 63 can be located and is physically sound, the information will be there as it was on the day it was published. Since this stability is demonstrably absent on the web, anticipated permanence of the information is an important criterion of judgement. Estimating the stability of a web site is problematic, closely related to authority, very important to libraries, and not yet resolved.

Evaluating WWW resources is also new to a degree in terms of the scale of the corpus of information being evaluated. An information explosion is occurring in all media. The explosion is dramatically apparent on the web due to its rapid, global linkage of wildly diverse files. Unstructured searches on general-purpose search engines return links to a vast number of documents, many of them worthless to the purpose in mind. Retrieval rates tend to be high, and relevance tends to be low. Improving search skills and using advanced search engines helps improve relevance, but only if documents worthy of research are available to be found. The need to sift the wheat from the chaff is not really new, but the ratio of chaff to wheat is especially high on the web.

The large number of publications that have not passed through traditional stages of quality control make judging the quality of resources both more necessary and more difficult. The World Wide Web enables self-published authors to bypass the traditional scholarly publishing process. To get a paper into a scholarly publication, an author must earn credentials, then write and rewrite in accord with standards imposed by editors, publishers, and peer reviewers. To become generally available to students, the scholarly publication must then be selected by libraries. Unlike the unorganized mass of information available on the web, a college library's collection represents a select portion of the corpus of published literature, selected for its appropriateness to research at that institution. Since most WWW resources bypass the traditional scholarly vetting process, selection is pushed down to the end user.

THE BEAUTY OF TRADITIONAL LIBRARY RESOURCES

Traditionally selected library resources are meant to reduce the chore of selecting worthy from unworthy documents. Despite the clear strengths of a carefully selected collection, it must be admitted that low quality resources have always been available in libraries. The vetting process of quality control is not perfect, and it does not always apply. For instance, ERIC documents have little more quality control than web pages. The Educational Resources Information Center (ERIC) makes documents outside the published literature available on microfiche. Their purpose is to provide easy access to theses, lesson plans, reports to school boards, and so on, that would otherwise be invisible, and therefore lost to most researchers. ERIC documents must be typed, and must be plausibly related to education, but little other quality control applies, and the documents are filmed as submitted. Like self-published web pages, they vary widely in quality. And also like web pages, some very valuable information that would otherwise be inaccessible is made available to interested readers.

Academic libraries may also subscribe to general interest items that are rarely acceptable for scholarly research. Professors assigning papers find, perhaps to their dismay, that they must often specify that *People* magazine is not an acceptable source. Then again, for certain types of research, the content, layout, advertisements, or coverage of *People* or *Seventeen* could be totally appropriate. In a related vein, *Scientific American* may be appropriate for a freshman paper, but not for research in an upper-level class. But for the most part, the books and journals found in an academic library are intended to be used for scholarly research, or at least for college-level study.

A more intractable problem for librarians and scholars is bad information in putatively good publications. Scholarship relies on trust, trust that researchers will be honest with their data, not plagiarize, and give correct citations. Scholars are expected to mean what they say and say what they mean. Sokal's hoax was a very prominent violation of that trust, but his immediate admission and his reasons for pulling the hoax arguably make his violation tolerable. More insidious are undetected violations of scholarly trust perpetrated for reasons that have nothing to do with the pursuit of knowledge. Some of these will always slip through, and even the best efforts of authors, editors, reviewers, and collection development librarians make a guarantee of 100% accuracy in published information impossible.

The problem of substandard resources in the library is writ large on the web. Low quality resources in the library should be the exception—

an unavoidable, small portion of the collection. But low quality resources, judged from a scholar's frame of reference, are the norm on the web. High quality research on the WWW is the exception in the late 1990s, at least on pages available without a paid subscription. Traditional library functions and resources are essential as a counter to the lack of quality on the web, because examples of high quality must be available for students to learn the characteristics of good written research. Without traditional library selection and organization, students will have difficulty finding worthy examples by which web sites can be judged.

Good print collections also need to be available for students to learn which medium of information is most appropriate for a particular information need. As librarians (but not necessarily students and teachers) know, it is not true that "everything is on the web." It is also not true that web resources are necessarily too unreliable for research. Books have their place in research, journals have their place, as do manuscripts, films, recordings, and artifacts. Now the WWW has a place, too. Just because students may misuse the web is no reason to limit access to WWW sources. Librarians, working with teachers, have a duty to point students in the direction of worthwhile resources. The WWW Virtual Library is a good example of librarians steering students in fruitful directions. For an overview of its purpose and guidelines for its use, see *Information Quality WWW Virtual Library* (Ciolek, 1997).

STRATEGIES FOR NAVIGATING THE HURDLES

So, although teaching students to judge the quality of WWW resources is essential, the teachers tackling the job face a number of hurdles: students' limited background knowledge, teachers' overly optimistic assumptions about students' research abilities, the impossibility of defining a set of universally applicable criteria, the philosophical and practical difficulty of defining quality, and the vast, uncontrolled nature of the web. Despite a few genuinely new aspects of the World Wide Web's hypertext medium, evaluating the quality of web resources is essentially the application of old skills to a new medium. But even though evaluation skills are old to experienced researchers, they are new to novices. The advent of the WWW as a source of citable information has highlighted student inabilities to judge the quality of resources.

Student deficiencies are not new, but the vast, uncontrolled nature of the WWW cause a greater rate of inappropriate resource selection than occurred when students used only library collections. Despite the range of impediments discussed here to teaching students to effectively evaluate information sources, their ability to do so is central to their educational achievement, and must be pursued despite the obstacles. In practical terms, and based on the ideas presented here, what can be done to mitigate these difficulties?

For students to work within the scholarly frame of reference, they must understand what it is. When a teacher gives a research assignment the background knowledge needed to understand and evaluate the information to be cited should be clearly indicated. Examples of good information resources should be provided, along with the criteria by which they are judged. Teachers should also be aware of reading load, and make clear to students the expectations for the course. This does not mean reduce the load, it means make expectations clear. Finally, teachers should be familiar with web resources in their field, and share their findings with students. In general, teachers should clarify their expectations, avoid unfounded assumptions, point out examples of good and bad information, and explain their criteria of judgement.

For their part, students must make the effort to learn and work within the scholarly frame of reference. Student attitudes may clash with this expectation, but without immersion in scholarship, students will not learn to effectively judge the quality of information. Students should spend the time and effort to acquire background knowledge on a topic as the first step in any research project. Students need to work to understand the perspective of their teacher and the discipline he/she represents. As far as using the WWW for research, students must realize that the WWW has virtually no quality control, and that many resources are not worthy of research. Therefore, students should become proficient at using traditional library resources, not rely too much on the WWW, and know when to ask for help.

As the keepers of organized, reliable collections, librarians must continue to preserve and promote carefully selected information resources. And as always, librarians must provide guidance and support to patrons in many ways, including instruction sessions, reference desk help, printed guides, and point-of-use instruction. As the particular strengths of the WWW as an information resource become clearer over time, collection development should be adjusted to take advantage of the strengths, and to compensate for the weaknesses, of the WWW. Librarians should continue to select and organize reliable web resources, and promote the use of reliable resources by providing instruction and finding aids. Finally, since the web is stronger on recreational than on scholarly information, the role of general-interest, recreational materials in the library may need to be reexamined. If the purpose of an academic library's collection is to provide a corpus of reliable information worthy of scholarly research and against which other sources can be judged, the library may want to reduce recreational reading material, and collect only publications worthy of scholarly research.

REFERENCES

Annals of Improbable Research. (1997). *The Ig® Nobel Prize home page.* [On-line]. Available: http://www.eecs.harvard.edu/ig_nobel/.

Carver, R. (1982). Optimal rate of reading prose. *Reading research quarterly, 18,* 56-88.

Ciolek, T.M. (1997). *Information quality WWW Virtual Library: The internet guide to construction of quality online resources.* [On-line]. Available: http://www.ciolek.com/WWWVL-InfoQuality.html.

Harris, A. J., & Sipay, E.R. (1985). *How to increase reading ability* (8th ed.). New York: Longman.

Leckie, G. (1996). Desperately seeking citations: Uncovering faculty assumptions about the undergraduate research process. *Journal of academic librarianship, 22,* 201-208.

Payton, T. (1997). *Web evaluation for secondary grades* [On-line]. Available: http://www.siec.k12.in.us/~west/edu/rubric3.htm.

Pirsig, R. (1974). *Zen and the art of motorcycle maintenance: An inquiry into values.* New York: Morrow.

Sokal, A.D. (1996a). Transgressing the boundaries: Toward a transformative hermeneutics of quantum gravity. *Social Text, 46/47,* 217-252.

Sokal, A.D. (1996b). A physicist experiments with cultural studies. *Lingua Franca, 6,* 62-64.

Sokal, A.D. (1998). *What the* Social Text *affair does and does not prove. Critical Quarterly, 40*(2), 3-18

Vonnegut, B. (1975). Chicken plucking as measure of tornado wind speed. *Weatherwise, 28,* 217.

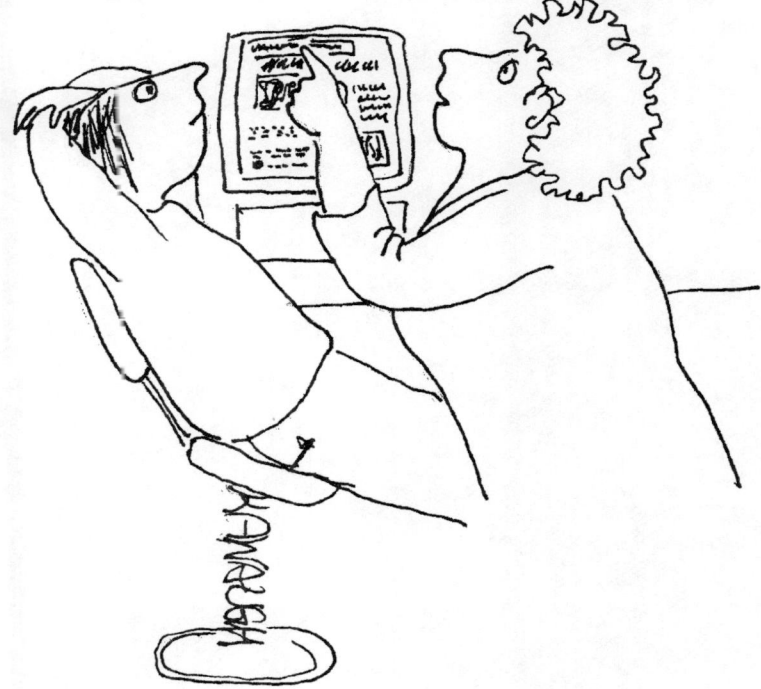
"serbianrevenge.com may contain a touch of bias"

EVALUTION WORKOUT
EXERCISES AND TECHNIQUES TO TEACH CRITICAL THINKING ABOUT WEB RESOURCES

Carol Doyle and Janet Martorana

ABSTRACT

The need for critical thinking in the web environment has been widely discussed, and there are many excellent resources which present criteria for evaluating information found on the web. In this paper, we identify problems caused by the web environment which can be alleviated by the application of critical thinking concepts to web information resources. We describe various types of activities in our instruction program, all of which contain some aspect of evaluation. We then give examples of evaluative exercises that we use in our quarter-long credit-bearing library courses, and techniques we use to insert similar critical thinking concepts into one-shot library sessions.

Critical evaluation of both the search for information and the resources retrieved is an integral component of library instruction programs and has received considerable attention in the professional literature. At the very least, for the same reasons we teach critical evaluation of other forms of information, we should apply critical thinking concepts to web information resources. As Hope Tillman states "we need to use the same critical evaluative skills in looking for information on the Internet that we would do in a book, a paper index, a musical score, or on an online commercial database."[1] The need to evaluate information found on the web is even more acute because of the ease of putting information on the web and the lack of clear demarcation between types of information. Information that is not reliable is more prevalent on the web than in published print materials, since much information on the web is not filtered, selected, reviewed or authenticated in the same way as is common for print information. It "bypass[es] many of the benefits of traditional publication—issuance by an authoritative source, editorial or peer review, evaluation by experts, etc."[2]

The greater allure and convenience of information on the web compounds the problem of the prevalence of unreliable information. Steven R. Knowlton notes in the *New York Times* that many educators "are concerned that the Internet makes readily available so much information, much of it unreliable, that students think research is far easier than it really is."[3] Librarians recognize the importance of teaching students to be discerning, knowledgeable information consumers. We work to increase awareness of the universe of information and teach the evaluative skills which can be used to identify the best and most relevant information resources.

SPECIFIC PROBLEMS

There are several problem areas unique to web resources which make the teaching of critical thinking and careful evaluation of vital importance:

- the ease and convenience of retrieving information—students are often disinclined to find better information elsewhere
- information overload—the problem of retrieving too much information without understanding how to sort through it or to focus the search
- the widely varying quality of information, often without clear indication as to the type of information (e.g., personal, entertainment, advertising)
- seamless connections to other information—following links from sites of known authorship or sponsorship can lead to information of lesser quality

- lack of overall organization of information on the web
- software or subscription requirements

EVALUATION CRITERIA

Numerous resources describe and discuss criteria for evaluating information found on the web. We take a holistic approach to the universe of information, integrating web information resources with other appropriate information resources regardless of form. We prefer not to treat the evaluation of information found on the web separately from the evaluation of other information, but to set out basic principles of evaluation which are applicable to any information resource. Authors who take this approach include Joni Kanzler, whose handout, "English 201—Evaluating Resources,"[4] emphasizes the continuity between the evaluation of print and web information. She outlines evaluation criteria for print resources, and then adapts them, adding a few additional criteria, to the evaluation of web resources. Another example is Julie Kwan's guide which doesn't differentiate between print and web resources, but gives criteria for evaluating "any new information resource."[5]

A particularly robust site that emphasizes continuity in the evaluation of print and web resources is Alexander and Tate's site, "Evaluating Web Resources."[6] Resources on this site outline the need for evaluation of the web; list criteria for print evaluation; adapt these criteria to web resources; and specify problem areas ("challenges") unique to the web, suggesting ways to address those challenges. This site also contains links to sites and pages that are examples of the different problems that the authors have discussed.

PURPOSE OF THE LIBRARY'S INSTRUCTION PROGRAM

The instruction program at the University of California, Santa Barbara (UCSB) Library has seven main objectives. These are to teach students:

- how information is produced and organized
- how to approach new information tools and resources
  - how to select appropriate tools to access information
  - how to effectively use access tools

- how to evaluate the search process and strategies
- to be aware of information resources in any form
- how to evaluate information resources and compare materials retrieved to select the most appropriate

Most of our formal instruction takes place in one of two hands-on library classrooms where participants can access the web and online databases. In a previous article, we discussed in greater detail the computer classroom and how we teach critical thinking in the electronic environment.[7]

We use a variety of methods to teach information literacy in our instruction program. Our basic approach is to integrate web resources with other information resources. In the different types of instructional activities, evaluative lessons are either implicitly embedded or explicitly conveyed. Types of instruction include:

- *Orientations*. These are usually general introductions to library resources and services, including hands-on access to web resources. They are targeted to specific groups of undergraduates or graduate students and faculty.
- *One-shot classes*. These instruction sessions are geared to specific undergraduate or graduate class assignments. Instruction in the library classrooms includes hands-on participation. Instruction in classrooms located outside of the library is provided through a combination of demonstration and lecture.
- *Quarter-long Library Skills (LS) classes*. These courses are designed to teach information literacy skills and research methods to undergraduate students. Students use web and print resources and online databases. They are asked to compare and evaluate various access tools and information resources.
- *Printed reference guides to subject resources*. These guides identify the major library resources in a discipline or on a topic, and include addresses to web resources.
- *InfoSurf subject pages*.[8] UCSB librarians select and provide organization to web resources through the development of subject web pages on InfoSurf, UCSB Library's website. Pages also link to html versions of the reference guides and Internet accessible subscription databases, integrating resources on a particular subject regardless of form.

- *Library tutorial on the web.*[9] The tutorial is used to reinforce instruction in the quarter-long library classes, as well as for independent learning. It provides instruction on how to use specific tools such as the library catalog, describes search techniques, and discusses criteria for the evaluation of resources.

EVALUATION EXERCISES AND TECHNIQUES

We have designed in-class activities and homework assignments for the quarter-long LS class which lead students to apply critical thinking concepts to web information resources. In the one-shot classes we have limited time to introduce research techniques tailored to the specific assignments. As it is not usually possible to make use of a full LS exercise in the one-shot classes or in orientations, we have developed techniques to work selective evaluative concepts into these sessions. In the following section we describe the exercises developed for the quarter-long LS class and give examples of how we address web resource evaluation in one-shot classes. The techniques we describe for one-shot classes can also be used to incorporate evaluation into orientation sessions. The exercises and techniques fall into two categories: (1) those in which we introduce and apply criteria to evaluate information resources, and (2) those that compare and contrast various types of information retrieved by different tools.

Introducing and Applying Criteria to Evaluate a Resource

Library Skills Class

Example 1: Making the link between citing and evaluating. This is the first exercise in the LS class that focuses on the web. It prepares students for later exercises specifically on web evaluation. In the exercise, students learn how to find elements they will need to cite web resources. These elements, such as authorship, sponsorship, and URL, are also key in assessing the value of a resource. Although the focus of this exercise is not evaluation per se, through class discussion we make the connection from citing to how these elements can be used in evaluating the usefulness of the information.

We ask the students to choose a topic from a list provided. We decide in class which subject page on InfoSurf they would use to find information on each topic on the list. We ask them to find a source relevant to their topic by following links off the selected InfoSurf subject page, and answer a set of questions regarding that source. The answers to these questions provide them with the basic elements for both citing and evaluating that resource. (See Appendix A for the specific assignment.)

Example 2: Identifying site affiliation as an evaluation tool. This exercise illustrates how identifying the sponsor of a site can help illuminate the context of an information resource, which helps determine its appropriateness. Students are directed to go to a web address where they find the following:

> And, it's all foolishness, anyway. The so called "global warming" scam is based on bad science and perpetrated by far-left control freak organizations that, for some reason, seem to be against human existence on this planet.[10]

This quote is from an article in the newsletter, *Heads Up*. The author and date are given but no other context (e.g., purpose or author affiliation) is provided in the newsletter. We show the students how to back up in the address which takes them to the homepage of the Michigan Militia Corps. Having identified the sponsor (or publisher) of the newsletter, the students can look at the other information on the site and ascertain the context of the newsletter.

Example 3: Using domain as an evaluation tool. Students are asked to go to two web sites that appear to be White House homepages: http://www.whitehouse.net and http://www.whitehouse.gov. When asked to identify which is the official White House site, students discover that neither provides a clear statement of who is responsible for the information. Examining the URLs, we point out that the "gov" domain indicates an official governmental site. We discuss various domains and their application to evaluation.

Example 4: Showing continuity between print and web resource evaluation. For this exercise, we distribute a handout describing criteria for the evaluation of both print and web resources. (See Appendix B.) The students are asked to read a brief article in *Time*[11] and an article on the same topic in the *New England Journal of Medicine*.[12] They answer a set of questions about each article, for instance, the credentials of the author, the intended audience, and whether it is primary or secondary source material. This segment of the exercise reinforces basic evaluative criteria in the familiar print environment and reminds students that there are different types of publications (e.g., popular and scholarly).

The second part of this assignment adapts the questions used to evaluate print resources to the evaluation of web resources. The students answer questions leading them to evaluate the information from two different websites on an endangered species, the Florida panther. Students discover that one of the sources is by two sixth grade students[13] and the other is by the U.S. Fish & Wildlife Service.[14] (See Appendix C for the assignment.)

One-Shot Classes

Example 1: Applying basic evaluative criteria. For a class doing research on the economics of natural resources, we used a search engine to search the boolean phrase "old growth" and "pacific northwest" and "logging." One of the resources retrieved was *Information About Old-Growth in the Pacific Northwest*.[15] At first glance, it has some good introductory information, and the class is asked to consider whether it is something they would use for their papers. In order to decide this, we suggest that they consider the same things they would use to determine appropriateness of a print source, such as a journal article. These would include who wrote it, when it was created, who published it, and its context (for what purpose it was written). In attempting to discover something about who created it, we find that neither author nor date is given. We back up in the address and discover that it is on a webserver at the University of Oregon which houses students' webpages. It is actually a term project for a forest biology class. We again ask them whether this is the sort of thing they would want to cite in their papers, since it would be like citing a friend's term paper who took the class last quarter. We reiterate the importance of investigating the information resources they find, by considering such things as context and authorship.

Example 2: Evaluating a source found through InfoSurf. A similar "teaching moment" popped up in an accounting class when we followed a link off of InfoSurf's accounting page, called *Corporate*

Information,[16] which connects to corporate information arranged by country. Several of the country sections have a link called "Accounting Overview," and we follow the link to Brazil's "Accounting Overview,"[17] as an example. The students are excited about the content so we ask them to determine whether this is a source their professor would consider appropriate were they to use it for their term paper. The source does identify the authors and date, but no other context is provided on the page. Backing up in the address, we discover that this is one in a group of term projects created and posted on the web by students in a class similar to theirs at Brigham Young University. Even though this information was found by following a link off our page, a link we selected because for the most part it connects to good information, when we evaluated it, it was found to be inappropriate for our use. This example illustrates the importance of evaluating every resource whether found through a search engine or by following links off of a known page.

Comparing and Contrasting Examples Between Information Retrieved from the Web and Journal Articles

Library Skills Class

The students are asked to search for information they would use to write a term paper about diet and its effects on health. They search both the web and the *Magazine & Journal Articles*™ database, a subscription database via the California Digital Library (CDL).[18] From each search, they are asked to select three to five relevant sources, and then from these, choose the best three. During class we discuss the overwhelming presence of advertisements for products and programs that were retrieved from their web searches on this topic, and that more appropriate material was found using the article database. The web search engines do not have a mechanism to either exclude advertisements or limit retrieval to more substantive information. Article indexes omit advertisements, and it is possible to target scholarly or more popular material by the index selected.

One-shot Classes

Example 1. The students are writing papers about professional ethics in accounting-related occupations. They first try using a web search engine to find information and get numerous hits, but few that are truly useful for their papers. We then take them into *ABI/Inform,*™ a subscription database available via the CDL, and find articles which discuss professional ethics issues in accounting. Some of the articles also mention the code of ethics of specific associations. We then show the class how to search the web to see if those associations and their codes are available. In this class, students discover that the information found in journal articles and the information they find on the web complement each other and are both useful for locating information they need for their term papers.

Example 2. In many classes, instructors direct their students to include several substantive articles on their topic in their list of references. We provide context to this requirement when we introduce selected index databases, by describing the type of information that can be found in articles. If other resources have been discussed in this session, we talk about how information in articles differs from information in the other resources. We also point out that these databases are available through subscription and are not accessible to non-campus users: what they are finding would not show up through a web search engine search, even though the database may be accessed through a web interface.

Comparing and Contrasting Examples Between Information Retrieved from the Web and the Library Catalog

Library Skills Class

Example 1. In this exercise, students compare and contrast information resulting from a search for books using the library's catalog, with a search on the web using a search engine. We ask them to search for information on the economic effects of global warming. Examining a book's table of contents that appears in the catalog record, we ask them to compare the depth and breadth of the subject's treatment in the book to that in the web source.

Example 2. This exercise shows how information retrieved by searching two different tools can complement each other. We ask students to select a book from a list we provide, and search the title of that book on the web and then in the library's catalog. The type of information retrieved via the web includes reviews, author information and bibliographies, and ordering information. They do not find the text of the book itself. The search in the library's catalog reveals that the book is available in the library.

One-shot Classes

During a presentation, we have found abstracts of U.S. Forest Service reports on the web. These abstracts link to information on how to order the reports, but the full text is not available on the web. We remind students that these reports might be available in the library. We then check the library's catalog and find that we do own these publications. We take this opportunity to show them what else they can find in the catalog. We have lured them into the catalog by finding a reference on the web to something they want, and then we show them what other related resources we have in the library. We point out that information found by searching the catalog complements and supplements the information found by searching the web.

Comparing and Contrasting Examples Between Information Retrieved from the Web and Other Library Resources

One-shot Classes

In a one-shot session for an accounting class, we illustrated the need to look in a variety of places to gather all of the information needed. We begin the session by using overhead transparencies to show the contents of a few basic print reference sources, and we demonstrate a CD-ROM containing corporate information. When we then examine selected free web resources that give current financial data, we compare what is available on those sites to the reference sources, which contain longer time series and more in-depth industry analysis. In order to perform their company and industry analysis, we point out to the students that they will need information from both the web and other resources.

CONCLUSION

Teaching the evaluation of web resources is integral to our instructional activities which are directed at promoting a greater understanding of the universe of information. The evaluation of web resources involves not only the examination of a specific resource, but also requires the awareness of other sources of information. Placing evaluation of web resources in this broader context enables students to identify the best information resources for their research needs.

We have described a variety of examples of how we teach the evaluation of web information resources. In the examples for the one-shot sessions, we have illustrated a general principle that we could call the "Johnny Appleseed approach," in which we try to take every opportunity to plant the seeds of why and how to evaluate. Using the same techniques illustrated in the examples, it is possible to tuck evaluative tidbits into orientations and even reference interactions.

APPENDIX A

INT 1 — LIBRARY SKILLS **Assignment 1: The Web**

A. Choose ONE of these topics. Place a 4   next to it.
    ___ You are writing a business plan for starting a business in California, and need information on the California economy
    ___ You need information on marine or aquatic science careers.
    ___ You are writing a paper on global warming for a class in Environmental Studies.

B. Which InfoSurf subject page is likely to have links to information on the topic?

C. Using links on that InfoSurf subject page, find a source which provides relevant information on your topic, and complete the information below for the source you found:

Title:

URL (Uniform Resource Locator = address):

Author(s):

Institution or organization sponsoring the website (if any):

Date(s) the information was created and/or posted (specify):

Quote a sentence or phrase from the page that directly relates to your topic:

Briefly discuss how the information you found will help you write a paper on your topic:

EXAMPLE

A student is researching the topic "Free Speech on the Internet," finds a useful source and writes it up as follows:

Which InfoSurf subject page is likely to have links to information on the topic?
> **Intellectual Freedom**

Title:
> **Fahrenheit 451.2: Is Cyberspace Burning? How Rating and Blocking Proposals May Torch Free Speech on the Internet**

URL (Uniform Resource Locator = address):
> **http://www.aclu.org/issues/cyber/burning.html**

Author(s):
> **Ann Beeson and Chris Hansen of the ACLU Legal Department and ACLU Associate Director Barry Steinhardt**

Sponsoring Institution or Organization:
> **The American Civil Liberties Union**

Date:
> **1997 (copyright date)**

Relevant quote:
> "... the Internet deserves the same high level of free speech protection afforded to books and other printed matter."

How it is of use:
> **This source addresses two free speech on the Internet issues, blocking software and ratings. It gives good background information on the topic, and is good example of the "pro-free speech" arguments. The ACLU website also has made links to other resources on free-speech that I can explore and potentially find additional useful information.**

APPENDIX B

Criteria for Evaluation of Resources
Which Resources Are "Good"?

Everyone has a bias, and all sources of information reflect the author's perspective on a topic. Before accepting information as truth, consider the following factors which will help you examine resources in terms of your own research needs:

- **Authorship**
  What are the author's credentials which gives credibility in this field? What is his/her area of expertise? Is the author affiliated with an organization or institution? If possible, try to determine the author's bias or perspective on the topic. Has he/she been cited in sources by others in the field? Biographical resources (e.g., *Who's Who* books, located in the library), and information in the publication itself, may help you determine the author's credentials.

- **Publisher/Journal**
  Identify the publisher and try to determine whether it is a reputable or scholarly publisher. If the information is in a serial, determine whether it is a scholarly journal or a popular magazine: who is the intended audience?; are sources of information cited?; are credentials of authors given?

- **Date of publication**
  When was the resource published? Do resources for your particular topic need to be current? Is the information contained in the resource current?

- **Content**
  Try to determine the purpose of the information and evidence of bias, its intended audience, its suitability for your purposes, and its comprehensiveness. Check for accuracy: can the information provided be verified elsewhere? Note whether the information is supported by evidence and appears to be valid.

- **Writing Style**
  How readable is the text? What is the purpose of the resource? Is it to entertain, to inform, or to promote a viewpoint? Is the information clearly presented?

Criteria for Evaluation of Resources on the Web

Just as print sources need to be examined for relevancy, accuracy and content, Internet sources also need to be examined for content evaluation in terms of your own research needs. Consider the following factors:

- **Authorship/source of webpage and content**
  What are the author's credentials in this field? What is his/her area of expertise? Charts, tables, text, bibliographies may indicate a particular agency or individual as authors or provide other citation information. The top or bottom of the webpage may identify an individual or institution who is responsible for the development and maintenance of the page: correspond with this contact if you want to verify the contents of the page or to make a suggestion or comment.

- **Address (URL, or Uniform Resource Locator)**
  Note the host computer type at the end of the computer address: e.g., edu, mil, gov, com. Site addresses which end in **mili**tary, **gov**ernment [non-profit] **org**anization or **edu**cation usually publish their own conference proceedings, statistics, newsletters, etc. Knowing an organization or institution's site address enables you to contact them to find the statistical methodologies used, survey techniques, and other criteria used in their research, and may give you an indication of their point of view, or bias.

- **Date**
  Check for a date when the webpage was created and/or last updated (usually at the bottom of the page). N.B.: Even though a webpage may have been recently updated, it doesn't necessarily mean the specific information you want has been recently updated!

- **Content**
  Some webpages will include a specific contents policy or information as to how the contents were developed, the methodology used, how often they're updated, the source of the contents etc. Try to determine the purpose of the webpage, its intended audience, its suitability for your purposes, and its comprehensiveness. Check for accuracy: can the information provided be verified elsewhere? Note whether the information is supported by evidence and appears to be valid.

- **Format**
  Is the information presented in an organized, logical manner? Is the resource simple to use and easily accessed? You may need special software or additional memory to load and make full use of the material presented at some sites: audio, moving images, sound, very large files.

APPENDIX C

INT 1 — LIBRARY SKILLS   **Assignment 7: Evaluation**

I. **Evaluating Journal Articles**
   You are writing a research paper on the association between coffee consumption and heart disease. You find the following two articles (copies attached). Evaluate the appropriateness of each article by answering the questions:

A. **"Comeback Time for Coffee"**
   1. Who authored this article and what are their credentials/area of expertise?
   2. What journal published this article?
   3. When was this article published?
   4. Is this article primary source material (results of research) or secondary source material (reporting on someone else's results of research)?
   5. Who is the intended audience for this article?
   6. Is the article comprehensive? Is there a bibliography for more information and/or to verify the information given?
   7. Do you feel confident that the information in this article is correct? Why or why not?
   8. From the answers you provided to the above questions, is the information from this article appropriate for your research? Explain why or why not:

B. **"Coffee, Caffeine, and Cardiovascular Disease in Men"**

   1. Who authored this article and what are their credentials/area of expertise?
   2. What journal published this article?
   3. When was this article published?

4. Is this article primary source material (results of research) or secondary source material (reporting on someone else's results of research)?
5. Who is the intended audience for this article?
6. Is the article comprehensive? Is there a bibliography for more information and/or to verify the information given?
7. Do you feel confident that the information in this article is correct? Why or why not?
8. From the answers you provided to the above questions, is the information from this article appropriate for your research? Explain why or why not:

II. Evaluating the Web for Research Information

You are writing a research paper on the Florida panther. You find the following two documents on the web. Go to the two documents and evaluate the appropriateness of each document by answering the questions:

A. http://www.indep.k12.mo.us/Elementary/procter/jclothier/Fpanther.html

1. Who authored this document and what are their credentials/area of expertise?
2. Who produced and/or sponsored this page? Is there contact information provided? Can you find more information about the sponsoring organization on the web?
3. When was this document created and/or updated?
4. Is this article primary source material (results of research) or secondary source material (reporting on someone else's results of research)?
5. Who is the intended audience for this information?
6. Is the information comprehensive? Is there a bibliography for more information and/or to verify the information given?
7. Do you feel confident that the information on this page is correct? Why or why not?
8. From the answers you provided to the above questions, is the information from this document appropriate for your research? Explain why or why not:

Evaluation Workout 51

B. http://www.fws.gov/r9endspp/i/a/saa05.html

1. Who authored this document and what are their credentials/area of expertise?
2. Who produced and/or sponsored this page? Is there contact information provided? Can you find more information about the sponsoring organization on the web?
3. When was this document created and/or updated?
4. Is this article primary source material (results of research) or secondary source material (reporting on someone else's results of research)?
5. Who is the intended audience for this information?
6. Is the information comprehensive? Is there a bibliography for more information and/or to verify the information given?
7. Do you feel confident that the information on this page is correct? Why or why not?
8. From the answers you provided to the above questions, is the information from this document appropriate for your research? Explain why or why not:

NOTES

1. Hope N. Tillman, *Evaluating Quality on the Net*. http://www.tiac.net/users/hope/findqual.html 1998. [Last accessed: 3/27/98.]
2. Scott D. Brandt, "Techman's TechPage: Evaluating Information on the Internet." *Computers in Libraries* 16 (April 1996):45.
3. Stephen R. Knowlton, "How Students Get Lost in Cyberspace" (Education Life Section). *New York Times*, November 2, 1997, p. 18.
4. Joni Kanzler, *Evaluating Resources Handout (English 201)*. http://www.library.bsu.edu/internal/ala/evalres.htm 1997. [Last accessed: 3/27/98.]
5. Julie Kwan, "Criteria for Evaluating Information Resources." *University Library Skill Guide*, No. 4, (The University Library, University of Southern California). http://www-lib.usc.edu/Info/Sci/pubs/criteval.html 1997. [Last accessed: 3/27/98.]
6. Jan Alexander and Marsha Tate, *Evaluating Web Resources* (Chester, PA: Wolfgram Memorial Library, Widener University). http://www2.widener.edu/Wolfgram-Memorial-Library/webeval.htm 1999 [Last accessed: 8/20/99.]
7. Janet Martorana and Carol Doyle, "Computers On, Critical Thinking Off: Challenges of Teaching in the Electronic Environment." *Research Strategies* 14 (Summer 1996):184-191.
8. Andrea Duda, *Resources by Subject*. http://www.library.ucsb.edu/subj 1997. [Last accessed: 3/27/98.]
9. Janet Martorana, *Library 101: Learn to Use the Library*. http://www.library.ucsb.edu/libinst/lib101/ 1998. [Last accessed: 3/27/98.]

10. Doug Fiedor, "A Loud 'No' to the Eco-Wackos." *Heads Up: A Weekly Edition of News from Around Our Country*, Issue 61 (November 30, 1997). http://militia.gen.mi.us/headsup/hu-61.htm [Last accessed: 3/27/98.]

11. "Comeback Time for Coffee: Let's Have Another Cup and Straighten This Out," *Time* 136 (October 22, 1990), p. 59.

12. Diederick E. Grobbee, Eric B. Rimm, Edward Giovannucci, Graham Colditz, Meir Stampfer, and Walter Willett, "Coffee, Caffeine and Cardiovascular Disease in Men." *New England Journal of Medicine* 323 (October 11, 1990):1026-1032.

13. Justin and Adam, *Florida Panther*. http://www.indep.k12.mo.us/Elementary/procter/jclothier/Fpanther.html [Last accessed 8/20/99.]

14. U.S. Fish and Wildlife Service, "Florida Panther: Felis concolor coryi (Bangs)." *Species Accounts*. http://www.fws.gov/r9endspp/i/a/saa05.html 1993. [Last accessed 3/27/98.]

15. *Information about Old-Growth in the Pacific Northwest*. http://gladstone.oregon.edu/~jcrant/intro.html [Last accessed 8/20/99.]

16. George Matthew Regnery, *Corporate Information*. http://www.corporateinformation.com/ 1998. [Last accessed: 3/27/98.]

17. Xin Wu, Michael Easton, David Williams, Antonio Urquiza, and Bryan Koehler, *Accounting in Brasil*. http://msm.byu.edu/c&i/cim/account/brazil/brazil.htm 1997. [Last accessed 3/27/98.]

18. California Digital Library. http://www.dbs.cdlib.org/ [Last accessed 8/20/99.]

A WEB PAGE IS NOT A PAGE:
EVALUATING DIGITAL INFORMATION

Hal Kirkwood and D. Scott Brandt

> *What misleads us is the inevitability of connecting the text to the drawing ... and the impossibility of defining a perspective that would let us say that the assertion is true, false or contradictory.*
> —*This Is Not a Pipe*, Michel Foucault

ABSTRACT

This chapter discusses the underlying concepts and interpretations of evalution in general and the evaluation of Web pages specifically. The importance and need for evalution and organization on the Web is argued. The authors review current methods of evalution and how the library profession must clarify and strengthen this as their role in the continually growing electronic information society.

Foucault's description of a painting by Magritte could also be applied to a Web page. With the Internet, we are often misled by the inevitability of connecting text to its container. In our case the canvas is an HTML document, which is kind of interesting when you consider how intangible such a container is—the record of civilization stored as so many electrons moving about on a network. This container which holds information can be as illusive as the meaning behind a surrealistic painting. The difficulty of finding a perspective with which to evaluate a Web page can seem equally impossible.

Evaluate. Validate. Value. Evaluation is the determination if something is real. It is the decision whether a thing is worthwhile. To determine this we must use objective criteria and methodology. We develop standards and compare things against them. Thus, evaluation is also the way we examine and judge something.

IN THE BEGINNING ...

As such, evaluation is nothing new. Modern day science is founded on objective examination, as prescribed in scientific method. In fact, every scholarly discipline has its standards for evaluation. Every major scholarly group, from the American Physical Society to the Modern Languages Association has a format which they require their authors to follow. It is ground into us as students in high school and college in the form of a term paper—expository writing backed up with facts. Validating. Ensuring value.

Thus, it all starts with the document, be that a print source or electronic source, such as a Web page. For the most part, there are two approaches to evaluation—ensure quality in a document before it is produced, or apply evaluation techniques and criteria after a document is produced. Basically, if information is rigorously reviewed, people can trust the source and accept an expert's assessment that it is valid and authoritative. When it isn't, they must assess and evaluate the information themselves. A review of these practices provides insight into evaluating digital information on the Internet.

Generally, material which is produced by a person or organization who is considered to be authoritative, expert and reliable is accepted at face value as being beyond refute. Information in a U.S. government document, for instance, has usually undergone careful research and attention to facts and details. The validity and reliability is rarely questioned, although reasons for the content may be (e.g., why did the government spend a million dollars on a thorough, authoritative report on whether frogs can be taught to talk?). And likewise, information issued from the American Medical Association or Chairman Alan Greenspan is likely to go without refute.

That is, such information is likely to be accepted without second thought if it is in print, or seen on television. These are mediums of delivery of information with which we are familiar, and in whose integrity we put our faith and trust. We believe our own eyes when we see it on television because such broadcasts have proven to be accurate—we know it is nearly impossible to "fake" transmissions (although remember, there was skepticism by some that the first walk on the moon was staged as a stunt). And much of the print media has achieved time honored reliability as well.

As students of the traditional publication process know, for hundreds of years, scholarly research literature has been produced in a precise and well structured way. The scientific method itself requires formal documentation of a detailed process of investigation. This structure for scientific or scholarly papers has required the author to think about what was to be presented, follow a format, and conform to prescribed standards to ensure quality. Other disciplines of study conform to similar rigorous practice. A newspaper's reputation is built on the integrity and reliability of its investigation and fact-gathering. In this way the originator of the document ensures that the content is validated. This adherence to such practice allows researchers such as physicists to share findings via "preprints" of papers which have been submitted to, but not yet published in, journals.[1]

But, even with the criteria and standards there to follow, rigor requires objectivity. So called "vanity" presses can allow anyone with enough money to publish a book, and tabloid newspaper magazines thrive on unsubstantiated information. The editorial and peer review processes have served to remove subjectivity and sensationalism from the publication process. Peer review requires a manuscript be reviewed by a number of specialists who are familiar with the topic or experts in similar areas. Peers review a document and give their expert opinion on the logic, methodology and content of a paper. In many instances, experts serve as a board of reviewers chosen by an editor. And in some instances the editor serves as the expert reviewer. The goal of such a process is to ensure validity and quality of the content of a document. (Ever wonder what a peer reviewed tabloid would be like?)

It is often not possible to have experts as reviewers judging a work. In fact, some works have little if any substantive review of the material before it's published. So how can the layperson put her or his faith into such material? It is critical that someone, somehow, review or assess materials. Several ways to accomplish this have been developed, such as review sources for books, core lists for journals. And librarians have been a critical and instrumental part of the assessment process with collection development policies, bibliographies, guides to specific literatures, and various types of resource reviews.

Librarians as a group have contributed in other ways, especially by creating mechanisms by which to organize material to make it is easier to deal with as part of a process. In fact, the discipline of librarianship is concerned with organizing information to make it easier to find and use, and to ensure access to valid, reliable information. The goal of cataloging, classification and indexing is to provide both a superstructure and an infrastructure for information. The superstructure is overarching organization and the rules of AACR2 and the MARC record structure represent the minute components which build an infrastructure. Only now are any highly structured mechanisms for organization being developed on and for the Web. One of some promise is the Dublin Core project, an approach to classification for Web pages.

AND THEN ALONG COMES THE WEB

Soon enough, the question that faces us is this: If Web pages are so different, do standard evaluation techniques apply to digital information sources? Physical documents—books, transcripts, journal articles—are supposed to be easy to evaluate. They are tangible. They are corporeal. They are self-incriminating. Web pages are not quite the physical entities that documents are. These documents on the Internet are like a sea of unfiltered information sources, mixed in with a growing number of reviewed materials. How do they differ from any other documents and how does that effect evaluation?

What is it that makes the Web page different? Is it because the Internet is a fairly new medium—that it isn't as familiar or commonplace as television or radio? Is it because the technology of the medium is new, and people don't understand how it works? (Do many people really understand how television works?!) Is it the problem that the Internet is an open system, which allows anyone to put up information, and that there isn't any reliable organization to it? These questions, and more, contribute to problems understanding Web pages, and more importantly the difficulty of sorting out, filtering, and evaluating information.

One problem is that a Web page is a representation. Mere electrons stored in one place, moved to another. Just as Magritte's painting states that a picture of a pipe is not a pipe, people are as easily taken back that a copy of Web page which is retrieved and viewed on a monitor is not THE original of an item, but a copy. Yet that copy is exact in every detail! It now sits on a machine where it can be altered, duplicated, and destroyed. A Web page is not actually the original of that document or file of information. It is an electronic copy. Not only can it change overnight, it can even change during transmission, if parts of the page don't load or are lost.

In addition to being electronic documents Web pages are curious devices in another way. They are filled with commands which we can not see which dictate how the document should look. As noted above from the discussion of televisions, we tend to believe what we see. But we can't see the HTML (hyper-text markup language) code which instructs a page to behave in a certain way—or as we'll see, how to be treated by search engines, and so on. And ironically, the hidden codes can sometimes affect retrieval, and ultimately influence how, why, and when to evaluate.

Another problem is that a Web page has no real formal structure for including or arranging content. It has very few limitations based on its format—it can be created by almost anyone and exist almost anywhere. A Web page does not have a definition. It can be a report, a picture, a list, an advertisement, or a single sentence. As such it is difficult to impose organization upon it. It is not easy to distinguish it from other forms of written communication, such as books, journals, newspapers, encyclopedias or theses. There are no directions or formats for writing a Web page as there are for print equivalents.

A Web page can be written by anybody. Even someone who does not have the skill or means to do so can have someone else do it for them. They are created by students, grandparents, amateurs, and professionals. Anyone with an idea, or just the urge to do so, can create a Web page. There is no application, no test, no reference check. No review of their credentials, background, or familiarity with the topic. And this can lead to spoofing—creating fake pages to mislead or entertain. As noted below, determining author identity is the most critical point of authentication, and the biggest need for evaluation.

And Web pages can cover any subject in any way. Given the option of adhering to notions of scientific discovery and rules of writing term paper or having free range over the page, it looks as though most people tend to follow their whims. A Web page is a canvas for expressing one's thoughts and opinions without necessarily checking them against reality. As a document, a Web page is more akin to a vanity press publication than any other form of communication—only there is no fee for publishing involved. This can make it particularly hard to build faith in the Internet as an information medium, when such pages become mixed in with the increasingly substantial documents being produced.

What does all this matter? Isn't that the point behind the Internet? That information should be free and available to all, and that all should be freely allowed to express their thoughts and feelings? Sure. The problem though is that the Internet is not simply an abstract medium of communication upon which we practice our First Amendment rights. It is also a physical medium of delivery of information. Because there is no infrastructure to help categorize, classify or structure information, almost every and any document has to be assumed unreviewed, unfiltered, and not validated.

THE NEED FOR ORGANIZATION

Likewise, because there is no overarching superstructure to organize information, we are faced with the compounded problem of not being able to clearly understand where a given Web page originates. If, for example, all Web pages were issued by an agency which authenticated them, we could have assurance. One source noted below offers a prototype for serving as a source that reviews pages. But those are few and far between right now on the Internet. This is due to the overwhelming number of pages on the Web, but is also due in part to organization which makes information retrieval so difficult.

Look at the composition of Web pages, how they're organized at Web sites, and how they end up indexed in search engines, the primary tools used to gather information on the Internet. It's easy to see how this entire process must make us focus on, and give importance to, evaluation.

The Dublin Core project (http://purl.org/dc/) mentioned above is one of the few attempts to bring sanity to the madness of overwhelming information on the Internet. It is not an attempt to ensure quality, but it seeks to bring much needed structure—a thesaurus for Web pages and guidelines for using them would go a long way to helping sort things out. Without some kind of special description, all pages are treated the same by search engines and it becomes very hard to sort them out from one another. Add to that confusion the fact that some pages don't even conform to the most minimal conventions of HTML coding. This is especially noted in the U.S. government's practice of putting documents on the Internet which don't have any HTML at all! Thus, even the simplest of search engines can do little with indexing and relevancy ranking with these documents.

Pages sit on servers that are wide open to anyone and anything to view. Automated programs (robots, agents, crawlers, or spiders) use the Internet's capabilities of networking and machine querying to identify, locate, and retrieve them. The selection can be comprehensive, but they are indiscriminate. For the most part, these programs can only pick up on how information is structured through HTML tags or words on the page. They can not distinguish between valid and invalid, accurate and false, important and insignificant. Relevancy ranking, while not an evaluation tool, is supposed to be an automated way of separating the cream from the crop—but as noted, pages themselves do not conform to any standard that would ensure effectiveness with ranking.

So called "subject directories" use human-mediated selection and can thus focus on context and meaning. Language, syntax and semantics are too complicated for the current generation of spiders to do much good in this regard. Thus, while search engines such as Yahoo are much smaller and selective than larger automated ones like Alta Vista, they provide a minimal level of filtering simply by exclusion. As more and more specialized search engines come out, perhaps library science and computer science can join hands to build evaluation into information technology.

But in the meantime, there are three traditional ways in which information is associated with quality. One, if it is written and/or issued by an authoritative source such as the federal government or a reliable organization, it is generally accepted at face value as having validity. Two, if it is authenticated as part of an editorial or peer review process by a publisher, it is generally accepted as reliable. Three, if it is evaluated by experts, reviewers, or subject specialists/librarians as part of collection development, it is generally accepted as authoritative. But how does this all apply to Web pages?

CONNECTING EVALUATION TO WEB PAGES

How shall we define evaluation? 1: to determine or fix the value of 2: to determine the significance, worth, or condition of usually by careful appraisal and study.[2]

The evaluation of World Wide Web sites is a real and definite challenge for librarians. As we have discussed previously the Web is a powerful new method of publishing. The ability for anyone and everyone to "put up" a Web site on their favorite topic or to express their own opinion is within easy reach. A global audience is but a click away. Librarians are uniquely positioned to bring a level of evaluation and clarity to the ever-expanding World Wide Web.

What do we mean when we say evaluation? We mean just what the definition says above, "determining the significance or worth of a site by careful appraisal and study." Librarians have been selecting, reviewing, and organizing information from the very beginnings of this profession. Librarians are trained to carefully appraise a source to determine its value and usefulness to fit our patrons' needs. The Internet and World Wide Web should not be looked at with fear or derision. There is a substantial amount of useless information, what T. Ciolek calls the impending "MultiMedia Mediocrity or MMM."[3] But there is a growing amount of high-quality research-oriented information. There is a need for someone experienced in the areas of selecting and reviewing information to separate the useful from the useless. The search engines currently available leave much to be desired in the way of truly accurate, manageable searches. They provide little, if any, information of an evaluative nature. The sites that claim to provide evaluative information are often sidetracked, or obsessed, with the buzzers and whistles, with what's "cool" about the site. Value and validity are rarely covered in the reviews. The impetus is left on the user to determine the value of the site. Librarians have attempted to stem the tide of poor decision-making by teaching and instructing users, patrons, and students in the necessary skills in evaluating electronic resources.[4] This is not enough. Librarians can use their expertise to create a greater demand and greater expectation for quality It is possible to create and implement criteria that will drive the creation and development of sites with strong responsible content.

Evaluating Digital Information 63

What are the areas of evaluative criteria? Evaluative criteria can be broken up into three general areas: objective, relative, and subjective. These three areas are all inter-related and contain a significant amount of overlap. Further discussion will be done in general terms and broad strokes to allow for clarity.

Objective criteria can be applied to almost every site or resource. These can be considered the standard issues when confronting a Web site: accuracy, authority of the author, currency, and comprehensiveness.[5]

Accuracy

- can be applied to the content as well as to the presentation,
- typos, incorrect grammar, and poor formatting,
- blatant mistakes, omissions of known fact.

Expertise and knowledge of a variety of sources in a variety of formats allows for a strong case to be made for librarians and information professionals stepping forward to bring order and accountability to the World Wide Web.

Authority

- is the author qualified to be presenting this information?
- what is the author's area of expertise?
- is the publisher related to the information in some way?
- do they have any interest, financial or otherwise, in projecting a specific agenda?
- has the information gone through any type of review process?

Knowledge of the methods of verifying the expertise of authors and publishers is not always available to the general public. Librarians can provide this expertise to assist patrons in making more informed decisions.

Currency

- is often more of an issue on the Internet than in other media,
- the low barrier or delay in the time to publication,
- users demand for immediate corrections and changes,

- peer or editorial review is often ignored or unavailable in the rush to publish,
- does the information seem current according to what you already know?
- is there any indication that the information may be dated?
- when was the site last updated?

Information professionals are capable of determining through comparison and experience with similar sources how current a site is and how appropriate it is that the information is served quickly. Often it is more valuable if the information is delayed due to some form of review process.

Completeness, Comprehensiveness, or Coverage

- does the site claim to be comprehensive?
- are there any indications that something is missing?
- comparison of the content of a site to other similar sites or to similar print resources

Sites that are projecting themselves as a research-quality resource should provide information on the material they are covering and elaborate on why information may, or may not, be available.

Relative criteria are based on need and can change as the topic of the site changes. Bias and audience can be considered relative criteria. It is important to determine if there is a bias on any site. Is the information being presented as fact or as opinion? The purpose of some sites is to influence or to promote a certain viewpoint. Is the bias clearly stated? Or is there a false objectivity being projected? Is the bias appropriate for the site? Perhaps the site is geared for a specific audience. Is this clearly obvious or explained? Is the information provided appropriate for the target audience? Criteria such as this will vary and change according to the user's perceptions and as the content and purpose of the site vary and change.

Subjective criteria vary according to the individual's choices and requirements at any given moment. If someone is looking for a site to apply to a university his or her criteria is an online application. If the need is commentary from right-wing point-of-view then that becomes the criteria. There are as many subjective criteria as there are information needs. Strongly related to relative criteria, subjective criteria will change according to the user's needs and the purpose of the site. The challenge is in providing enough information on a reviewed site that makes it apparent what the scope and content is to allow for informed decision-making.

DOING IT

People traditionally evaluate something every day of their lives. Deciding what to watch on television, choosing between products at the grocery store, or selecting which way to go to work are all potential moments for evaluation. As we discussed earlier it is determining the value or worth of something through careful appraisal. Over time certain choices become second nature due to repetition and consistent results. But initially there was a moment of appraisal. There is the inherent bias between Republicans and Democrats. The belief that certain publications are more accurate or trustworthy than others is pervasive.

Television shows are now rated on content for the purpose of parental control of what their kids are watching. *Time* magazine is more trusted than the *National Enquirer*. But what happens when the *National Enquirer* breaks a real story ahead of the more trusted news magazines? Was your perception of *Time* magazine different after careful appraisal and review of the faulty and inaccurate study on Internet pornography was published? When NBC's "Dateline" program was accused of staging explosions on trucks, without informing the viewers of this, how did this impact the evaluation of this news show? Are viewers now more skeptical of the show? Are they evaluating the information more stringently because of this apparent lie?

The Web is no different. Generally there is a quick evaluation of a site and then a belief that the site will always fulfill the necessary information need. As information professionals we must apply criteria all of the time and must avoid the trap of becoming comfortable with our initial evaluation. There is a need for constant and repetitive evaluation of constantly changing Web sites. How do you evaluate and compare the Time Pathfinder site to the MSNBC site to the Drudge Report site? All of these could potentially be truthful and accurate resources for information. They can be potentially biased sites as well. It is the librarian's job to assist users in judging the information found on sites and in resources. The creation of criteria and the careful development of a selection process are just two of the ways that we add value to the information we serve to our users. On the Web there are projects under way that are doing this same type of value-added evaluation.

HOW OTHERS DO IT

The Web is awash in evaluative directories. Many are focused on the concept of what is "cool." There is little differentiation between personal, commercial, research, and propaganda sites. The important criteria is how visually appealing or how unique the buzzers and whistles are on a given site. Little, if any, space is given to truly evaluating the content and the author.

Magellan (http://magellan.excite.com/) is one of the better known directories of rated sites. Recently purchased by Excite, Inc. Magellan is in the process of an editorial transition and is not adding any new sites nor updating any current reviews. The current method of review consisted of a brief descriptive paragraph and a rating from one to four red stars.

An example of a review:

> Live From the Hubble Space Telescope Webchat
>
> Review: The title is a bit misleading, as this is an area for folks to use to talk up the Hubble—it ain't actually originating out in space. Anyway, pick a handle and hopefully someone else will be online.

This site received three stars on the Magellan scale. No information is provided on the reviewer and the review itself leaves much to be desired in the way of evaluative or informative information. The focus is not on the site as a whole, just on the chat portion. The Magellan site does not provide easy access to information concerning the inclusion of the sites nor the amount of sites available.

In comparison the Encyclopedia Britannica (http:www.britannica.com/) is providing access to its Internet Guide of 65,000 sites classified, rated (on a three star scale) and reviewed. Britannica provides a page that details the selection criteria and the method of evaluation of the sites. A user can obtain a clear understanding of what will be included and what will not in the Internet Guide.

The same site as above reviewed by Britannica:

Live from the Hubble Space Telescope

NASA

Component of the Passport to Knowledge project to create "electronic field trips to scientific frontiers" for K-12 students. Includes summaries of three interactive telecasts in which the students and scientists discussed observations of Neptune and Pluto. Additional features are students' project-related artwork, "puzzlers," an online forum, an archive of Q&A among students and HST team members, a teacher's guide, a chat room and discussion group, a gallery of astronomical images, and a directory of other astronomy-related sites. This resource showcases how the Web, videoconferencing, e-mail, discussion groups, etc., can be used to enhance science education.

This site rated two stars on Britannica's scale. This review is a much more informative review than the Magellan version. The focus is much more scholarly and research-oriented. This is to be expected from a more historically trusted source like the Britannica. As in the case of determining the authority of the author of a Web site it is just as important to determine the authority of the reviewers.

These are two sites that evaluate a large number of sites in a wide and varied amount of topics. The desired purpose is to serve anyone and everyone. They both have advantages and disadvantages depending on the user's needs it is apparent that they will also fall short of meeting their desired purpose. They will also fall far short of including every relevant site on any given topic.

Narrowly focused sites are now sprouting up on the Web. This is where the real power of evaluation takes place. Groups of specialists in given areas carefully and thoughtfully select sites to add to a subject specific guide.

Examples of this include the Marr/Kirkwood Official Guide to Business School Webs (http://www.bschool.com/) and the Blue Web'n (http://www.kn.pacbell.com/,wired/bluewebn/) guide to learning sites. These sites each focus on a specific area and use a unique method of presentation. The Marr/Kirkwood site uses tables and detailed criteria to allow for easy comparison between business schools. Breakdowns by country and athletic conference are also available. The tables are configured to allow for linking directly to that specific section of the site. A more detailed review including a rating on a five star scale and a descriptive paragraph is also available. This site is beginning to drive the development and enhancement of business school Web sites due to its constantly changing and adapting criteria.

Blue Web'n, on the other hand, provides reviews on a five star criteria and a brief description similar to the larger evaluative sites. The difference here is that the focus is on learning and education. Sites are classified by Dewey Decimal subject areas, as well as by a content table where subjects can be cross-matched with topics like tutorials, lesson plans, and Web-based projects. As does the Marr/Kirkwood site, the Blue Web'n site provides a detailed description of the rating criteria and the purpose of the site.

These sites are creating a value-added service for Internet users by sharing the expertise of the reviewers. The careful appraisal by knowledgeable specialists in focused areas is a useful and important area for information professionals to pursue on the Internet. An increase in the amount of collaboration is necessary to push the Web toward the development of more useful resources and sites. Librarians can put themselves in a position to positively influence the value and accountability of Web site development through the careful and thoughtful evaluation of sites.

A HOPEFUL FUTURE

Though Web pages themselves may be different from print documents in their structure and volatility, they share with documents the need for evaluation and the need for a process to deal with them. On the one hand, we need internal mechanisms of organization and structure. A thesaurus of descriptive terms is the kind of approach that can help. Educating people on standards for layout and content is another. On the other hand, external evaluation is likely to be needed for a long time. Just as likely is the need for people, experienced, trained, knowledgeable people, to conduct the evaluation. Until (or if) we can achieve the same kind of success and sustainability with peer and editorial review we have with print, we will continue to need to focus on evaluation for Web pages in practicing and in preaching.

NOTES

1. R.T. Bottle, 1973. "Scientists, Information Transfer and Literature Characteristics." *Journal of Documentation* 29(3):281-294.

2. Merriam-Webster WWW Dictionary. 10th ed. http://www.m-w.com/netdict.htm [July 30, 1998].

3. T. Matthew Ciolek. "Today's WWW, Tomorrow's MMM: The Specter of Multi-Media Mediocrity." *Educom Review* 32(3) May/June 1997. http://www.educom.edu/web/pubs/review/reviewArticles/32323.html [July 30, 1998].

4. Marsha Tate and Jan Alexander. "Teaching Critical Evaluation Skills for World Wide Web Resources." (includes informational Web page checklist) *Computers in Libraries* 16(10) November-December 1996, 49-54.

5. Adapted from Judy Pask, Roberta Kramer, and Scott Mandernack, *The Savvy Student's Guide to Library Research.* West Lafayette, IN: Purdue University Undergraduate Library, 1993.

EVALUATING WWW INFORMATION:
INSTRUCTION METHODS IN THE ELECTRONIC CLASSROOM

Jennifer Dorner and Susan Taylor

ABSTRACT

Learning how to evaluate information sources has always been an important part of a student's education. Yet this ability to judge the value of information sources is a skill that takes time and experience to develop. Students who cannot differentiate between good and bad resources in the library cannot be expected to tell the difference on the World Wide Web, when, for the first time, they are faced with the sole responsibility of determining the value of the information in a source. Instructional Services at the Ball State University Libraries has recognized this and has long been educating students in two electronic classrooms about the types of information available on the Web and how to choose resources appropriately. Depending on time constraints, the needs of the professor, and the type of class, one of several instruction techniques is used. This chapter discusses the following teaching methods used at Ball State related to evaluation criteria: a brief introduction, an individual exercise, a group exercise, a workshop, and a Web exercise.

Learning how to evaluate information sources has always been an important part of a student's education. Anyone who has tried to convince a student not to use a paid advertisement section of a magazine as a source for their research paper knows that students do not always recognize the difference between trustworthy and questionable information and that this ability to judge the value of information sources is a skill that takes time and experience to develop.

The library provides a kind of safety net for researchers. The materials included in the library are primarily sources developed through traditional print publishing which requires that information meet a set of standards. Not all publishers adhere to these standards, but generally they do manage to screen out dubious works. Those works that make it to publication are further scrutinized under the editorial process, which attempts to eliminate any errors that may exist in the manuscript. Through the collection development process, librarians play a further role in screening the resources. Comparing the works to others on the same topic, and checking the credentials of the creators, librarians attempt to guarantee that the resources included in the collection can be used with impunity.

Students are generally unaware of the effects of the filtering process that occur in the print publishing industry. Having not yet learned that there are varying levels of value among information resources, students may not recognize that Internet information does not always live up to print publishing standards.

And why should the student go to the library when, according to the media, a vast universe of information is accessible through his home computer? It is usually only the information professionals who find it satisfying to answer an information need with a trusted print reference resource rather than with a dubious World Wide Web site. For students, whose grasp of information literacy is shaky at best, the Internet with its graphics and its hype, is a much more appealing tool.

These students who cannot differentiate between good and bad resources in the library cannot be expected to tell the difference on the World Wide Web. The Web is the world's largest vanity press with anyone having access to a server able to publish. And publish they do—from collections of recipes and ideas for world peace to gossip about the stars. Even the contents of an individual's desk has been immortalized at a Web site. The variety of content is only equaled by the variety of usefulness.

That is not to say that excellent resources are not available on the Internet. Stock quotes, government publications, consumer information, and weather bulletins are just a tiny portion of the information that is being accessed by individuals every minute. The new accessibility of "grey" literature, previously published as pamphlets, preprints, and conference proceedings, is another example of the usefulness of the World Wide Web (Tillman, 1997). Associations and organizations now have a cheap and easy means to disseminate this valuable information. Even resources like Medline, previously available only through commercial services, are being made available on the Web.

WWW information is not stratified into classes of quality, however, and a tool is yet to be developed that can help searchers sort the good from the bad. Subject archives such as Yahoo or Magellan may attempt to categorize and even evaluate Web sites, but they can only handle a small fraction of what is being published. Even those sites that provide ratings often focus on the "coolness" of a site and "tend to omit consideration of issues of content and authority with which librarians are more concerned" (Smith, 1997, paragraph 21). Even less effective are search engines, which cannot discriminate at all between "useful" and "useless" information. A student using the search terms "Civil War" is just as likely to find a site entitled *My Civil War Ancestors* as he is a site entitled *Civil War History*. Even more confusing to students is determining the difference between two sites entitled *Civil War History*, one of which is put together by the National Archives and one by a Civil War buff.

With the advent of the World Wide Web, students now are faced with the sole responsibility of determining the value of the information in a source. Instructional Services at the Ball State University Libraries has recognized this and has educated students about the types of information available on the Web and how to choose resources appropriately for as long as they have been providing instruction on the World Wide Web. Ball State faculty have seen that many students are making unwise choices about their use of WWW resources and have accordingly increased their requests for library instruction in the evaluation of Web resources.

The methods for providing instruction are outlined later in this chapter. All of them address certain criteria that the Instruction Librarians have determined to be significant. To apply these criteria evenly across the spectrum of materials available on the World Wide

Web is next to impossible. E-journals, articles, searchable databases, resource guides, and newsgroup postings cannot all be judged using the same standards, just as various resources in the library—online databases, CD-ROMs, periodicals and reference books—are not all judged by the same exact standards. But even the non-specific guidelines we provide for appraising the contents of a Web site are of some value to the students, if only to show them that this evaluation process needs to occur.

EVALUATION CRITERIA

The seven evaluation criteria outlined below are not the only ones that can be applied to Web sites, but they do serve to point out to students the most important aspects that should be considered before blindly accepting the information provided at a site and including it as a research source. Additionally, a healthy dose of common sense should be applied when evaluating a Web site.

Scope

Most reference resources include a statement by the author or editor that explains the work's scope—its breadth and comprehensiveness. Internet sites which do not explain their scope are likely to waste the time of the searcher, who may be looking through a site for information that is not there. Sometimes the scope is only implied or can be inferred from a table of contents or an index, but the best sites will include some explanation of their contents and how extensive they are.

The site should explain what aspects of the subject are covered and whether the resource is focused on a narrow area or includes related topics. It should describe what level of detail is provided about the subject and whether the information is limited to certain time periods.

Sites authored by organizations often include a mission statement, which should not be confused with a statement of scope. The mission statement provides the purpose of the organization. It might include descriptions of activities and services that are not at all reflected in the contents of the Web site.

Audience

Determining the intended audience will assist the user in judging whether the content of the site is appropriate for his purposes. A WWW legal site written for the layperson might be useful to someone looking for simple definitions of legal terms, yet of limited usefulness to the legal professional doing research. If the site is directed towards a specific audience, then the content of the site should be appropriate for that audience.

Authority

Authoring takes many forms on the Internet; an author can be an individual, an organization, company, or government agency—just about anyone. Identifying the author is an important step in evaluating the Web site. Anonymity on the World Wide Web is not a positive indicator of the validity of the information; if the author is unwilling to be identified, then the information should be suspect.

It is also vital to look for information on the author's credentials. The author's education, training, or experience in a field relevant to the information should be explained at the site. If not, other sources should be consulted to find out more about the author.

Another factor to take into account is that the person or group of people who created the Web site might not be responsible for all of the content. For example, it is possible to create a page that is a compilation of article reprints by various authors. To cite one of these articles in a paper, it would be necessary to know who wrote that particular article, not who created the Web site.

Currency

It is always a good sign when a date appears on a web page indicating that the page has been updated or modified recently. This shows that the site is at least still active. But that date usually provides no information about what specific change was made. The author may have revised the content of the page, added content, or simply changed the color of the text. The date does not necessarily reflect when the content was created.

Even more troubling is the fact that the information itself on various Web pages is frequently not dated. At a site on diabetes that was updated a few weeks previously it may be possible to find an article on a treatment method for diabetes. If the article itself is not dated, how would it be possible to determine when the information was created? If the information was 20 years old, it would certainly be of no use to the reader. Providing this vital piece of information is often overlooked by Web authors and can cause great difficulty for researchers.

Accuracy

As mentioned at the beginning of this chapter, most print resources go through a screening process where they are critiqued by an editorial or peer review board or evaluated by experts, reviewers, subject specialists, or librarians. Web resources rarely have editors or fact-checkers who review the information before it is published. And at this time, no Web standards exist to ensure accuracy.

Determining accuracy of Web information is a daunting task. To conclusively determine accuracy one would have to compare the information at the Web site to reliable information published elsewhere, somewhat defeating the purpose of using the Web at all. As an alternative to that extreme measure, it is possible to look for clues that will indicate accuracy. One sign is whether the author refers to and/or demonstrates knowledge of the literature on the subject. The author may demonstrate this by referring to related sources. If so, the sources should be documented. Documentation of the information provided is very important. If an author doesn't support his facts—especially quoted statistics—with the source of the information, then that information should be suspect. Also, if the author of the information is well-known and considered trustworthy then the information presented is likely to be accurate.

Purpose

It is rare that the goals of the author are stated up front at a Web site. Sometimes these goals are obvious: the author wants to inform, to persuade the reader, or to sell something. And, as many Web sites serve only as a vanity press for the author, there may be no purpose to the site other than to serve as a soap box or to show off an author's design abilities.

Identifying the site's agenda or purpose helps the student to determine whether a bias is present. Remember the student who could not differentiate between an article and a paid advertising section in a magazine? Now that student is faced with a new type of publication on the Web—the infamous "infommercial," a company site that is a mixture of informative content and advertising. Recognizing that the content on such sites is designed to influence the audience to purchase a product should suggest to the user a possible bias in the information.

Organization, Structure, and Design

The design of a site may not be relevant to the quality of the content, but how easy it is to navigate the site is important. Sites that have too many graphics and are slow to load on the computer screen can cause great frustration. Sites that are too visually confusing or "busy" make locating information difficult. Also, the organization of the site and clarity of the directions for operating it is vital to ease of use.

The pages should show their relation to each other, using common design elements and directional cues. From each page one should be able to get back to the home page. This is important because a search engine or another site may provide an address to a page within a Web site that is not the home page. Since it is easier to navigate a site from the home page, that link to the home page is important.

Web browsers support different versions of HTML, the language used to write Web pages, and Web pages should be written so they can be clearly viewed by every type of browser. Text-only versions of the pages should be provided by the authors for those using text-based Web browsers.

While not all of these design elements will matter to the user interested only in the value of the information, clear organization of a Web site will engender more trust in it as it indicates that care has been taken with the site.

INSTRUCTION METHODS IN THE ELECTRONIC CLASSROOM

At the University Libraries at Ball State, we have two electronic classrooms featuring state-of-the-art technology. We will refer to these rooms as Classroom 1 and Classroom 2. Classroom 1, which came up in the fall of 1995, has an instructor station with demonstration capabilities as well as the LINK System which provides the instructor with complete control over the monitor, keyboard and mouse of each of the 26 student terminals. All terminals have access to the library's catalog, CD-ROMs, and the Internet, and the student desks are arranged in rows. Classroom 2 was brought up in the summer of 1997 and is nearly identical to Classroom 1 as far as equipment is concerned. However, the student desks in Classroom 2 are grouped into "pods" of six to eight terminals.

The electronic classrooms allow us to teach Internet research skills in a manner that encourages active learning by the participants. In the library instruction program at Ball State, we have been making every effort to include evaluation of Web resources when we discuss searching the Internet. Depending on time constraints, the needs of the professor, and the type of class, we select one of several instruction techniques which follow.

The Brief Introduction

Quite often professors ask us to give their students a brief introduction to the WWW, in addition to the list of other databases and sources they would like to have demonstrated during the instruction session. Naturally, this does not allow us much time to talk about evaluation, but we do consider it vital to bring up the topic. After having gone over subject archives and search engines, we remind students that they need to cite what they choose to use from the Internet. This allows us a good opportunity to discuss why they should use Internet information cautiously.

We have found that for nearly every situation, it is useful to begin the evaluation discussion by showing the students an example of a poor Web site. We often show a humorous, fraudulent site first, and then move on to a site with erroneous information which has potentially harmful consequences (such as incorrect medical information). This brings home to the students the fact that it is dangerous to use information without assessing the reliability of its content. Appendix C provides a list of questionable Web sites which help librarians provoke reflection by the audience on why evaluation is important. If time permits, we show them examples of misleading or inaccurate Web sites, and then go over the evaluation criteria, referring to the handout (see Appendix A). This method is used when time is the most constrained.

Individual Exercise

If an entire period is devoted to Internet searching, then there is often time to work in an evaluation exercise. With some groups of students individual work seems the most appropriate. After showing them a fraudulent site and going over the evaluation criteria, we may ask students to complete the evaluation worksheet (see Appendix B) for a Web site which we provide. The Web site to be judged should be related to the topic the students are studying. Sometimes professors can help provide suggested links or the names of related professional associations which may have home pages. The best sites for them to examine are those which may have some very good features, but which are questionable in some way. If the students are able to learn that "all that glitters" is not good content, we feel we have reached them. After they have had five to ten minutes to complete the worksheet, we try to facilitate some discussion related to what they have learned. We have found it easier to guide the exchange if students have been evaluating sites which we have had a chance to look at ourselves.

Group Exercise

Many of the regularly scheduled library instruction sessions at Ball State are 50 minutes long, but there are some classes that last 75 minutes. For those, there is often enough time to utilize the pod arrangement in Classroom 2 to have the students complete the evaluation exercise (Appendix B) as a group. The library instructor first presents the criteria, demonstrating their application by using Web site examples for each. Then one pre-selected Web site is assigned to each pod. One person from the group is elected as the reporter. The group is then given some time to examine their Web site, attempting to answer the prompting questions on the reverse side (Appendix A), which the reporter records.

After about 10 minutes, each reporter in turn discusses the findings of his or her group. The student indicates whether the group was able to locate the information that provided them with the answers they needed. If so, the students consider what the answers they found say about the quality of the information at the site. Finally the group is asked to state whether, after this process, they would feel comfortable using this site as a source of information for their research.

Workshop

The ideal situation for teaching evaluation techniques and skills is a workshop devoted to that topic. We have offered several 90-minute workshops entitled "Evaluating WWW Resources" to faculty in the past year and a half. They have been well attended, proving that faculty are becoming more concerned with the quality of information on the Internet. The format for these workshops has varied somewhat, and will no doubt continue to change as we come up with other ideas to make the instruction meaningful.

Typically we begin in the same manner as our other instruction evaluation sessions; namely, we show a couple of poor WWW sites, one of which is humorous and the other of which is on a more serious topic. Next we go through each of the evaluation criteria, discussing each in relation to traditional library resources, such as books and journal articles. A slide presentation helps to highlight the salient features of each of the criteria. Then we look at each of the criteria as it pertains to the World Wide Web, making suggestions as to what to look for on a Web page. We display Web pages which are either poor or excellent for each criterion.

We encourage questions along the way and increasingly hear stories from faculty of student papers which have been based on weak information from the Internet. To get the faculty more involved, we next ask the participants to choose one of four Web sites (which we have already examined) and to analyze how well it covers each of the criteria using the evaluation worksheet (see Appendix B) as a guide. It is important to discuss with them what they discovered. Beyond asking about each of the criteria, we ask when they would feel comfortable using the information on that site, if ever. Would they want their students to use that material in an academic paper?

Teaching a workshop as opposed to a class gives a different tenor to the session. Those who show up for a workshop are there because they want to be. They are interested in the topic and want to learn more. Students who are brought over to the library for instruction by their professor may or may not be interested and motivated to participate. We have found that graduate students are definitely more engaged than undergraduates.

In preparing exercises for an instruction session, we have found that we feel less comfortable assigning faculty a specific exercise to complete. We tend to give them more open-ended activities so that they have room to explore as they see fit. When our audience is students, we feel we can be more exacting in what we ask of them, particularly if we have the open support of the professor.

A Web Exercise

Another method for teaching evaluation skills grew out of two successful library instruction sessions for Dr. Hodson-Carlton, a professor at Ball State's Nursing school. Two of her courses (one undergraduate and one graduate-level) focus on the use of computers in nursing practice and the impact of the Internet on the health care profession. The library instruction sessions provided to these classes were similar to the format of the "Evaluating WWW Resources" workshops offered to faculty, but the evaluation exercise was completed by groups. This exercise was particularly effective with these students, who immediately saw the implication for their practice.

The quality of medical information on the Internet is of special concern to these students who recognize that the promulgation of unscreened and unfiltered health care information can be dangerous to consumers. One group of researchers studied over 40 Web sites which addressed treating fever in children and found that only a few gave accurate and complete information. They concluded that this "suggests that there is an urgent need to check public-oriented healthcare information on the Internet for accuracy, completeness and consistency" (Impicciatore et al., 1997, paragraph 30).

After these library instruction sessions were held, Dr. Hodson-Carlton approached Instructional Services with a request to develop a WWW evaluation module that could be integrated into her course Web site for the graduate-level class. Using a combination of HTML documents and tests created with inQSit (a testing tool developed by Ball State's University Computing Services), the module was created to provide the same information covered in the library instruction sessions. After each criteria was listed, a link to an exercise was given. The student was required to follow that link and answer questions based on the information they could find at a pre-selected health care Web site. A mixture of good and bad Web sites were used as examples. The module was finished in early February 1998 and was put to use by the graduate class a few weeks later.

PARTICIPANTS' REACTIONS

When participants in a library instruction session or workshop are asked to review a site and evaluate it, the students and the library instructors generally arrive at the same negative or positive conclusions about the sites. Almost always the negative decisions are reached because of the lack of information available at the site to answer the students' questions about the criteria. They begin to mistrust the sites that won't provide this type of information up front.

For the nursing students who completed the web exercise, almost all of them indicated that they found the process of evaluating WWW information to be difficult, but that when they applied the criteria, many of the health care information Web sites came up short. The activity was a revelation for a few students, who stated that sites previously visited and used by them would have to be reevaluated, based on what they learned from the module.

FUTURE PLANS

In the upcoming year we plan to put together a Web tutorial, covering Internet search techniques, with students in a required freshmen English class as our target audience. We will include a section on the evaluation of what they find on the World Wide Web. Since this tutorial will be required of all freshmen, it gives us an excellent opportunity to instill evaluation skills in all Ball State students early in their college career.

CONCLUSION

The electronic classroom environment provides students with the opportunity to immediately put into practice what they have learned about evaluation. Having the appropriate equipment available in the classroom allows students to apply the criteria directly after hearing about them, a method of learning far superior to the traditional lecture.

There are additional benefits to group work, which permits the students to share their experiences and ask questions of each other that they may not feel comfortable asking the instructor. Verbalizing their findings during the discussion similarly strengthens the learning experience.

These discussions have shown that once the students are required to examine Web resources using the same type of criteria used to judge print resources, their previous opinions about the general usefulness of Web resources are always revised. Without the active learning exercise and the subsequent discussion, the impact of instruction would be greatly diminished.

APPENDIX A

Evaluating World Wide Web Information

Scope
    Subject: What is it about?
    Depth: How detailed is it?
    Coverage: Is the subject limited to certain time periods?
    Comprehensiveness: Is this *everything* on the topic?
    Does the information accurately portray the subject, or is there information missing?
    Format: Are only certain resources included, i.e. only WWW sites, only telnet, newsgroups, etc?

Audience
    For whom is the page written? Children? Adults? Scholars?
    Is the content appropriate for the intended audience?

Authority
    Who wrote the page?
    What are their credentials? Are they experts?

Currency
    Is the information up to date?

Is it consistently being updated?
Is timeliness important to the subject area?

Accuracy
Is there a bias present? Is it stated or not?
Is the information correct?
What is the source of this information?

Purpose
What is the purpose of the resource? To Entertain? Inform? Teach?
Is the purpose stated?
Does the resource fulfill its purpose?

Organization, Structure, and Design
Is the page easy to understand and use?
Is it organized in a way appropriate for the content and purpose?
Are the graphics meaningful? Do they need to be?
Are there too many graphics, making it difficult to load?

APPENDIX B

Evaluation Sheet

Title of WWW page: _____
URL: _____

Scope: _____
_____
_____
_____

Audience: _____
_____

Authority:
  Author: _____
    Expertise/Credentials: _____

Currency: _____
_____
_____

Last update: _____

Accuracy: _____
_____
_____

Purpose: _____
_____
_____
_____

Organization, Structure & Design: _____
_____
_____

APPENDIX C

SCOPE
Good: US Patent & Trademark Office http://patents.uspto.gov/
Bad: Tech Encyclopedia http://www.techweb.com/encyclopedia/defineterm.cgi

AUDIENCE
Good: Girl Power! http://www.health.org/gpower/index.htm
Bad: The Sociology Corner http://www.sociology.net/index.html

AUTHORITY
Good: National Institute for Health http://www.nih.gov/
Bad: Diabetes Information Page http://www.geocities.com/Athens/Forum/5769/diabete.html

CURRENCY
Good: National Science Foundation http://www.nsf.gov/
Bad: Anywho Toll-Free Internet Directory http://www.tollfree.att.net/forms/tf.html

ACCURACY
Good: U.S. Census Bureau http://www.census.gov/
Bad: Facts About Growth Hormone http://www.cosmicdome.com/health/
The American Smokers' Alliance http://www.smokers.org/
Harry V. Martin's Free America http://www.sonic.net/sentinel/

PURPOSE
Good: EDGAR http://www.sec.gov/edaux/wedgar.htm
Bad: Melatonin Central http://www.melatonin.com/

ORGANIZATION
Good: Yahoo! http://www.yahoo.com/
Bad: 'Lectric Law Library's Reference Room http://www.lectlaw.com/re‾.html

FAKE SITES:
DreamTech International http://www.d-b.net/dti/
Feline Reactions to Bearded Men http://www.improb.com/airchives/cat.html
Mankato home page http://www.lme.mankato.msus.edu/mankato/mankato.html
White House http://www.whitehouse.net

REFERENCES

Impicciatore, Piero. Chiara Pandolfini, Nicola Casella and Maurizio Bonati. (1997, June 28). Reliability of health information for the public on the world wide web: Systematic survey of advice on managing fever in children at home. BMJ [Online], 314, 33 paragraphs. Available: http://www.bmj.com/bmj/archive/7098ip1.htm [1997 November 20].

Smith, Alastair G. (1997). Testing the surf: Criteria for evaluating Internet information resources. The Public-Access Computer Systems Review [Online], 8, 65 paragraphs. Available: http://info.lib.uh.edu/pr/v8/n3/smit8n3.html [1997, December 10].

Tillman, Hope N. (1997). Evaluating quality on the net. [Online]. Available http://www.tiac.net/users/hope/findqual.html [1997, December 10].

A RENAISSANCE IN EVALUATION SKILLS:
TEACHING STUDENTS TO EVALUATE INFORMATION RESOURCES IN A GENERAL EDUCATION PROGRAM

Trudi E. Jacobson

ABSTRACT

Project Renaissance, a pilot general education program at the University at Albany, provides the opportunity for librarians to teach students the basic components of information literacy: the ability to find, evaluate, and use information sources. The project has a strong focus on technology, particularly the Internet. Librarians work to combat student over-reliance on web-based resources by teaching information evaluation skills in a variety of innovative ways.

Students today face an overwhelming array of information sources. When this choice is combined with the typical undergraduate tendency to do research at the last possible moment, it leads to a preference for finding the most easily available information sources. The result is not academically ideal. The guidance professors provide on the research process is often given after the fact, once students have turned in their completed papers. Librarians have the opportunity to provide input at an earlier stage. They are able, both during the reference encounter and during course-related instruction, to encourage students to consider the sources of the information they use.

PROJECT RENAISSANCE

Since the fall of 1996, librarians at the University at Albany have had an ideal opportunity to teach students the importance of information evaluation through a pilot general education program. Administrators and faculty members created Project Renaissance in order to provide a small college feeling for freshmen at the university. Project Renaissance made this environment possible for 200 students during the 1996-1997 academic year. These freshmen lived together in one dormitory quadrangle, sharing two adjoining buildings. They took six credits of general education courses in common during each of their first two semesters. The Project Renaissance courses, both in lecture format and small group discussion, focus on the theme of human identity and technology. Student access to and use of computer technology is a key component of Project Renaissance. Students participate in a service learning program, and attend cultural events with their classmates. Librarians play an integral role in the program: they introduce students to the core components of information literacy: the ability to find, evaluate, and use information sources.

The program had been on the drawing board for two years prior to its debut in the fall of 1996. It was during the initial planning stage that the University Library became a core component of the program. Early involvement was crucial for successfully integrating librarian participation into this general education effort. The idea that was to become Project Renaissance first surfaced during the work of a committee that was investigating the establishment of a teaching center on campus. A librarian was a member of that committee, and was able to advocate for library participation once the program began to assume its shape. The chair of this planning committee, and later the first director of the new Center for Excellence in Teaching and Learning, was also convinced of the importance of including a librarian as one of the core faculty members for the project. While librarian participation in this general education program was almost a foregone conclusion, librarians at other institutions have developed strategic campaigns to insure that information literacy components were included in their general education curriculums (Reynolds 1989; Sonntag and Ohr 1996).

Project Renaissance doubled to 400 students during the 1997-1998 academic year, and will expand to 600 students in 1998-1999. The initial components of the program have stayed essentially the same as it expands. Each year, the students are divided into teams of approximately 100 students. These teams attend lectures together, but are subdivided into discussion sections of 15-20 students. Librarians teach the students in these smaller configurations.

The Project Librarian participates in a two week summer planning meeting each year. She meets with the project faculty members and teaching assistants as a group, to inform them of the potential instruction sessions available from librarians. After years of publicizing our instruction program, it was surprising to find that some faculty members were completely unaware of it. As a result, outreach efforts beyond this program have been increased. The Project Librarian is available to consult with the teaching teams as they construct their syllabi and develop course activities, in case they have questions about research assignments or other library-related matters.

In the two years of the program, librarians have taught classes covering the online catalog, electronic databases, basic web navigation, subject-related resources, and the evaluation of information. One unusual feature of the library instruction provided to Project Renaissance classes during its initial two years, in comparison to that provided to general education programs at some other universities and colleges, is the flexible nature of the content. Faculty members and teaching assistants are informed of the variety of sessions available to them, but they are able to choose which segments best meet the needs of their students and assignments. They are also able to work with the Project Librarian or bibliographers to develop very specialized sessions. Only a very few discussion sections have opted not to have any instruction. Most teaching assistants have requested from two to four different classes. Almost all the instruction is requested for the fall semester. Unfortunately, this flexibility will not be possible once the Project grows to 600 students. Two core sessions, one on the online catalog and electronic databases, and the other on the evaluation of information, will be offered to each section. Elective sessions will only be possible during the spring semester, when the instruction load is lighter.

FOCUS ON TECHNOLOGY

A key component of Project Renaissance is the use of technology. The aim is for all participating students to gain an introductory level of computer literacy that they can draw upon during college and in the workplace. Many of the students have their own computers, with access to campus resources through the ResNet program. ResNet enables students to connect directly to library, computing, and academic resources. Students without their own computers can use workstations in the user room in their dorm. The Project uses computer conferencing software so that students become comfortable with the computer as a writing and communication tool. Students are taught to use Internet technology such as e-mail, listservs, news groups, and the World Wide Web. There is a web site for the project itself (http://www.albany.edu/projren/), and students either develop their own web sites or work on a class web site. During the 1995-1996 academic year, one team developed a Virtual Museum of the 20th Century. One set of students identified key people, events, organizations, and cultural artifacts to display on the virtual museum web page, after which a research team contributed explanatory blurbs on each "exhibit." However it is used, technology pervades Project Renaissance.

This focus has its benefits. Students quickly become familiar with a variety of software packages and computer uses. Only the rare student seems hesitant to use technology. Students are introduced to the need to reflect on the role of technology in society. However, from a librarian's point of view, the particular emphasis on the World Wide Web impedes student awareness of the full range of information sources available to them, and of the need to critically evaluate the information they do find.

EVALUATION OF INFORMATION CLASSES

Librarians have been addressing the need to teach students to evaluate information sources, particularly information obtained through the Internet, at conferences, both in formal sessions and informal discussions, in articles, and on web sites and listservs. Tate and Alexander's article (1996) lays out quite clearly some of the important criteria that students need to consider when evaluating web pages, including accuracy, authority, objectivity, currency, coverage. Hahn (1997) provides an annotated bibliography of articles, web sites and other resources that discuss the evaluation of information found on the Internet.

University at Albany librarians have taught sessions targeted to the evaluation of print and electronic information sources since the spring of 1996, and it was a natural development to make this a key component of the instruction offered to Project Renaissance students. Due to the focus on electronic resources in the Project's courses, we highlight Internet site evaluation in these sessions. We have found these classes to be among the most rewarding ones that we teach, because they allow us the option to be creative and because we can see students connecting with the material immediately. Both classes described below are taught in hands-on classrooms.

THE FAKE WEB PAGE CLASS

One of the classes that several librarians have taught involves the use of a fake web page that the author and the Network Services Librarian, Laura Cohen, developed. This page is a pseudo-bibliography, with annotations, on the topic of the psychosocial parameters of Internet addiction (http //www.albany.edu/library/internet/addiction.html). It combines real article citations and web sites with others that were the product of our imaginations. These phantom citations to articles, reports, and web sites contain clues as to their nature. Linking pages contain a brief biography of the bibliography's "author," an explanation of the purpose of the page, and a page indicating which citations are real and which are not (developed for other educators and librarians around the country who are using this page in their classes).

The librarian asks students to work in pairs during this exercise. They are instructed to work their way through the items in the bibliography in order to figure out how they might find them in the library or access them. This calls upon skills they gained in previous instruction sessions, and also does not give the game away. As they begin to read through the items, they are at first intrigued by the Internet addiction topic (perhaps it hits close to home?), and then skeptical as they read some of the annotations. Asking them to work in pairs is to encourage them to learn from each other, though this often works better in theory than in practice. When they are all sitting in front of their own computers, the temptation is to work at one's own pace. Occasionally a student will understand the true nature of the exercise right away, but generally the students don't.

If one does catch on quickly, he or she is encouraged to keep the knowledge secret, until the rest of the class catches up.

Students are next asked to go to the page with the information on the author. This is a slightly skewed faculty biography, and students start to point out the anomalies. By now there is generally a fair amount of suspicion about the web site, and the librarian admits that they have been looking at a phony page. Rather than explain to students why they have been using this web site, the librarian asks them the reason, to encourage them to think about it. The librarian then begins an item by item discussion, in which students need to explain whether they believe each article or web site is authentic. At this point, students don't need much prompting to evaluate the listed web sites to which they have been able to link. They appear to grasp quickly the need to analyze the discrete pieces of information, at least on this page, but it is only following the discussion that there is widespread understanding of the implications of anybody being able to mount anything on the web.

Following this exercise, the librarian passes out and discusses with the class a list of criteria to use when evaluating web sites (http://www.albany.edu/library/internet/evaluate.html). She also asks them to consider the same issues of authority, accuracy, and timeliness when using more traditional sources, which frequently will lead to a discussion on the topic.

COMPARING PRINT AND WEB-BASED RESOURCES

The Project Librarian developed another exercise for use in a Project Renaissance section where there was the opportunity to give students homework before they arrived in the library. This exercise asked students to compare one or two traditional reference sources with a web site on the same topic. Students were given the list of resources they should examine a week before they came to the library. Due to miscommunication on the part of their teaching assistant, very few actually did this homework (she mistakenly assigned it as extra credit work). It was possible to salvage this class by asking students to work in small groups for part of the class time, comparing the reference materials the librarian brought to class with the web sites. This approach has since worked well with other classes that did not have time to prepare before class. The topics of these resources were: Biographical Sources, Holocaust, Nuclear Warfare, and Greatest Movies. (See appendix.) In one case

(Biographical Sources), the print and electronic sources were directly comparable. In the other three cases, the resources had different focuses. Each group reported on their findings to the class as a whole, taking into consideration who was responsible for each source, what authority they have, if there was evidence of bias, and when the information was published/updated. Most groups noted that there were differences in intent between the resources, and the revisionist history web site was identified as such. In some groups, students felt the electronic resource was superior, but they provided reasons for their opinion. Students were surprised to discover the range of traditional reference materials available to them, a product, undoubtedly, of our emphasis on electronic tools in our instruction sessions.

The interest level in both of the classes described is uniformly higher than in other sessions for these students. Once they become engaged in the subject they are examining during class, they do translate some of their enthusiasm to evaluating the source of the subject material. They are able to use their computer skills while adding to their knowledge base, though there are always a few students who are tempted to use the opportunity of having a high end computer in front of them for searching their own topics.

One of the teaching assistants who has asked a librarian each year to teach her students about the evaluation of information comments, "I found this type of class very useful and extremely important for college students who are relying more and more on electronic information. Personally, I never questioned the credibility of the sources when I sought information on the Web until I heard the librarian the first time. Now I've gotten into the habit of looking at the builder of the page every time I see something new and I also keep telling my students about that. It is wonderful that we have such convenient access to an enormous amount of information, but isn't it scary to think that rumors or false information get spread so easily and so quickly just because people take things for granted or they just get too busy sorting out what they see and forget to check where they originated?" During one semester, this teaching assistant only required students to use web-based resources for their class. They did not have to use any print materials at all. After she sat in on the evaluation of information class and became aware of some of the issues surrounding materials mounted on the Web, she changed the policy for the class, an immediate and gratifying result of an instruction session.

APPENDIX

Project Renaissance Assignment

DATE DUE: October 29, 1997 During Class

Listed below are printed and web-based sources for four topics. You are to compare the printed and web-based sources for each topic. For each source, answer the following questions:

1. Who wrote and/or published this information?
2. What authority do they have?
3. Is there any evidence of bias?
4. When was the source published or last updated? Does this have an effect on the information?

Be prepared to discuss in class your comparison of the sources for the four topics.

TOPICS
1. Biographical Sources
   Biography
      www.biography.com/find/find.html
   Chalmers General Biographical Dictionary
      Ref CT 102 N45 1969 (32 vol)
   Cambridge Biographical Encyclopedia
      Ref CT 103 C26 1994

2. Holocaust
   Remarkable Nonsense About the Holocaust
      http://members.aol.com/ihrgreg/nonsensense/nonsense.html
   Encyclopedia of the Holocaust
      Ref D 804.3 E53 1990 (4 vol)

3. Nuclear Warfare
   Documentation and Diagrams of the Atomic Bomb
      www.netsurf.org/~dimitri/atomic.html
   Penguin Encyclopedia of Modern Warfare
      Ref U 27 M33x 1991 (See entry on Atom bomb)
   Nuclear Almanac
      Ref UG 1282 A8 N9 1984

4. Greatest Movies
   One Hundred Greatest Films
      www.filmsite.org/momentsindx.html
   Academy Awards Index
      Ref FN 1993.92 S53 1993

Please leave the books used in this assignment on the shelf when you are done looking at them, so everyone will have a chance to find the materials. Thank you.

REFERENCES

Hahn, Susan E. 1997. "Internet: Let the User Beware." *Reference Services Review* 25 (Summer): 7-13.
Reynolds, Judy. 1989. "University Approval of Library Research Skills as Part of the General Education Curriculum." *Reference Librarian* 24: 75-86.
Sonntag, Gabriela, and Donna M. Ohr. 1996. "The Development of a Lower-Division, General Education, Course-Integrated Information Literacy Program." *College & Research Libraries* 57 (July): 331-338.
Tate, Marsha, and Jan Alexander. 1996. "Teaching Critical Evaluation Skills for World Wide Web Resources." *Computers in Libraries* 16 (November/December): 49-55.

TEACH THEM TO FISH IN A DIGITIZED AND NON-DIGITIZED ENVIRONMENT:
DEMYSTIFYING PRINT SOURCES TO CREATE A BALANCE BETWEEN THE ELECTRONIC AND TRADITIONAL ENVIRONMENTS

Bennie P. Robinson

ABSTRACT

Today students enter college with an awareness of the superhighway, the internet, and the world wide web with some experience in using them. They also come with the misguided notion that everything needed for their research purposes is available in cyberspace and can be retrieved in a few seconds at any time repeatedly. This easy access to information through ever evolving technology has de-emphasized the importance of printed resources to last resort choices or unaware resources. This dilemma has created a need for instruction librarians to work in both the digitized and non-digitized environments to help students create the necessary balance for success.

Give a man a fish, and you feed him for a day.
Teach a man to fish, and you feed him for a lifetime.

—Chinese proverb

As we enter the new millennium, librarians, user instruction librarians, in particular, are responsible for ensuring that library users are both information and computer literate so they can function to their fullest capabilities now and in the future. Today one cannot read the newspaper, listen to a radio broadcast, or watch television without reading something about the Internet. Sometimes URL's are provided during a program, extending an invitation to visit the sites. These invitations advertise the new technology to consumers as often and in as many different ways as possible.

The implementation of President Clinton's vision to connect everyone–every library (public, school, college, special and hospital) to the information superhighway and the funding to provide and support it, the cooperative programs between some colleges and high schools to bridge the gap between high school and college, and the increase of ownership of personal computers[1] has extended the awareness to the Internet. These numbers are growing every day. According to an Internet survey as of January 1998: "29,670,000 Internet domains exist; an increase over the January 1997 figure of 16,146,000.[2] Therefore, students who enter college today have been introduced to the Internet and the WWW before their arrival on a college campus, bringing with them the notion that cyberspace contains everything important and necessary for research. This notion, created by cyber-technology, has created the need for instruction librarians to connect the "MTV" and "Nintendo" generation, now possessing an instant gratification syndrome, to a more rigorous research process and the traditional research sources available beyond the Internet.

The Internet is a huge, unorganized, unstable place, making it difficult to locate the exact information you need when you want it.[3] If, indeed the information you seek is actually there. The Internet is not located in one specific place; it has homes all across the world. The Internet does not operate under the same rules as other electronic information systems you may use (your OPAC and CD-ROMs), making for confusion as one moves from one to the other. The Internet has no shape or boundaries and is constantly growing. The speed of change on it can be instantaneous.[4] You can perform various actions to locate information on the Internet:

Digitized and Non-Digitized Environments

(1) you can browse;
(2) you can search by subject categories;
(3) you can search using one of the many available search engines;
(4) you can search by using an address (URL) for a specific site.

Most sites provide links within them to other related documents or web sites. When you do not have a specific URL, a search engine may be the answer. One of my students this semester shared her experiences on the Web, she was seeking the web site for the White House. After selecting a search engine, she entered her search terms, "white house." She received a huge number of responses, discovering upon examination that a large number of them were false. One hit in particular, included a white house, but not the one at 1600 Pennsylvania Avenue in Washington, D.C. She also received matches on sites that could not be related to her search term at all. Pages out of context could not be traced back to the original full document.

Another student shared his experience when he went back to revisit a site from a previous week's work. The famous "404 error" message which means "no web page could be found with the name specified could be located." The volatility of this environment meant something to this student at that point!

The Internet has no comprehensive index covering the variety of information it encompasses. It has no single starting point. You cannot rely on a list of web sites since they may go out of date quickly. You cannot rely on particular features of a search program, since they change constantly as new features are developed and implemented.[5] Each search engine has a different combination of features, seemingly making it so no one search engine can or will find everything you are seeking. A student must use several search engines for the same search and then, must select what is most appropriate for them.

Criteria to help the students determine what is most appropriate are:

(1) Accuracy, reliability and error free;
(2) Authenticity: who is the author? What qualifies that person to build a site on this subject?
(3) Objectivity: is the information presented with minimum bias? Is there an attempt to sway one's opinion?
(4) Coverage: what is the breadth and depth of the information?

(5) Currency: how current is the information? Is the the date it was posted to the Web clearly stated?
(6) Copyright: Is the material on the web site copyrighted and is the owner of the copyright indicated?

A student can spend a lot of time evaluating the resources located on the Web, sometimes finding that the catch of the day is not as large as expected. In a world where productivity and speed are emphasized, spending hours determining the reliability of one's research does not seem profitable. The fishing has great promise, a possible feast, but only a few herrings may be in the net, possibly to be thrown back in the water. Like a professional researcher, students need to be able to fish in the sea of information and catch protein-rich data with having to cast and recast their nets,[7] without having to toss back most of their catch. Finding research results that are of poor quality, irrelevant, not timely, inaccurate and lacking authority, makes continuing that activity a struggle.

Anyone with access to the Internet and some HTML experience can publish on the WWW. There is no peer review before that publication process. There is no verification of facts, no one to check for inaccuracies, no one to enforce that these authors be honest and responsible in what they are placing for all to read. Many authors are irresponsible, not having observed the principles of the culture of printing or publishing.[8]

Students easily master the skill of point and click to navigate through the Internet, but are less likely to master the skill that will allow them to become critical consumers of the vast amount of information at their disposal. Librarians, in collaboration with faculty, must provide students with the evaluation criteria, and provide sessions in which they can practice this skill.

Another factor causing concern is the possible cost involved. When users find full-text information on the WWW, there is sometimes a handsome fee involved to get the information. For example, a student writing a paper, did her research on her computer at home. She found three articles that appeared in a management training journal. One article was eight pages long; the second was six pages in length; and the third was just five pages. The cost to print them from that web site seemed so prohibitive to the student that she actually came to the library, located the print issues, and photocopied the three articles at a fraction of the cost. In this examples, access versus ownership did not ease any burden for the user.

These costs also emphasize the budget constraints that all types of libraries feel these days. Vendors providing the access to these electronic resources have not reduced the high cost of this information. Colleges and universities, looking to split the costs, have formed consortia to help defray or lower the price in some manner. Unfortunately at the time of renewal, these costs often double and even triple. Publishing is a business and profits must be made for the vendors to stay in business, but the cost of providing this electronic access frustrates those who handle the budgets at educational institutions. The demand for these resources is great, but the funds to pay for them are increasing to meet the demand. Each time a book or journal is sold, it provides income for someone and makes important information available to the society at large. The dream or myth that all books and journal articles, past and future, will be digitized, is a farce. The cost would be prohibitive. It is untrue that Project Gutenberg is digitizing comprehensively to provide free resources to the public. What has been digitized so far is free, assuming one has the hardware and software needed to access it. Only materials that are beyond the copyright limitation have been digitized to date. The resources most needed by students and researchers are copyrighted and not available on the WWW.

The Internet has some good qualities. It allows users to search other library catalogs (colleges, university, public and national catalogs) around the world. Business have discovered to be a wonderful new territory for advertising and sales. The speed with which one can locate information is also a plus.

As a result of the flaws mentioned previously, the Internet has lost a bit of its luster. Librarians Crawford and Gorman,[9] Oberman,[10] and Stoll,[11] though not a librarian but one of the pioneers in the online world who has joined the librarians in concern about the Internet. Stoll states that librarians and teachers alike are rushing blindly to promote the usage of computers and the Internet in the classroom. He says this is not because it needs to be done, but simply because it can be done. This use of the Internet de-emphasizes studying and promotes usage of limited resources that allow the cutting and pasting of information to pass as research. Some teachers think that using computers is the greatest thing since sliced bread, and other think like Stoll. David Rothenberg, an associate professor of philosophy at the New Jersey Institute of

Technology, agrees with Stoll. He says that the Internet has contributed to the decline in the quality of student research, something he has been observing in his students' assignments from year to year. He also observes that the students' attention span has shortened and their reasoning ability has declined.[13] My colleagues and I at this university have observed that students limit their research to only the full-text information available from the WWW, giving no consideration to what they are acquiring and whether or not it is appropriate for their research needs.

Libraries are a legacy to today's generation, providing the heritage of the past and promise for the future. Since the inception of libraries, the professionals within them have selected and collected millions of books, manuscripts and journals, amassing large collections. The items in these collections were written by experts, reviewed by the peers of those experts, and have had the facts contained within them checked for accuracy. Although the Internet has approximately 45 million web pages (as flashed across my screen while searching using Excite), libraries contain much, much more. This, in itself, indicates that the largest source of information to date is in print, on paper, and that the Internet has the capability of only complementing the traditional library.[14, 15]

Tools have been designed to bring together information seekers and information sources in the traditional environment. Complex classification systems organize books on the shelves, controlled vocabulary allows information seekers to search for the information contained on these shelves and in these books. Journals and newspapers both have tools to allow searchers to get to the right place at the right time. Indices and abstracts, both general and specific subject-oriented, have been designed to provide access to their content by subject, author, and title. Electronic versions permit keyword searching and advanced concept searching where one can include more than one subject or term together in a search, using Boolean and proximity statements to focus the searches.

Students who enter college today have been saturated with television and computers. They have a cursory knowledge and experience with the traditional library. They need to be introduced to the many resources available in print, and instruction in how to use them. Through seminars and tutorials on library instruction, available in class sessions and through a library's web page, students are introduced to these sources and the manner in which to use them. Students are taught first:

- to clearly identify their information needs, translation that need into a question
- to identify the appropriate terminology to be used in the search
- to identify alternative terminology
- to formulate a search strategy, constructing and defining a search statement
- to match these subject needs with the appropriate resources

The next step is to provide the students with evaluative criteria that will help them assess the resources they locate. These criteria, for the traditional print as well as the electronic materials, were mentioned earlier.

First, students are directed to use the local online catalog to find books and other resources available within their home institution. When the material they need is unavailable, they check the OhioLINK central catalog (a union catalog of approximately 50 colleges and universities in the states of Ohio) to determine if an institution in the state owns what they need. A student can request the material online through this central catalog if it is available. If not, a student must use the traditional interlibrary loan network, which is by no means as fast as OhioLINK.

Next, students are instructed in the use of indices and abstracts for their field of study. Using electronic indexes and searching by keyword will bring the students relevant material plus many false hits. The student must hone their evaluation skills to separate the good hits from the false ones.

Next, the student is shown how to use the WWW to find information to supplement and complement their research, Many professors are now asking that their students use only the WWW for their research, indicating that the faculty, too, need instruction on the wealth of information available in print form. However, if this is the instruction given to the students by their faculty, the librarians must help the students make the most of that resource.

To accommodate the variety of learning styles, pathfinders on various topics are provided to the classes. These pathfinders have the following components:

- a list of possible subject headings that might be useful in finding information
- a list of the possible indices and abstracts on a course topic
- a list of the journals in the library that covers the course topic
- a list of research tools, such as encyclopedias, dictionaries, and so on, that cover the course topic
- a list of Internet sites with URLs

The flaws in the WWW are not so significant that librarians write it off. It is improving all the time, especially as librarians design tools to help organize and search it. Librarians must use it and teach its use in a judicious manner.

Despite the changes in the library as a result of the new technology, the mission of the library is the same—to develop self-sufficient life-long learners and to ensure that they have access to opinions, and information they need to function effectively and enjoyably, regardless of the format in which the resources are packaged. A choice does not have to be made between print and electronic. Instead, it becomes a matter of integrating the old and the new to provide the highest quality, fastest and least expensive access to resources for the community it serves.

APPENDIX

Library Exercise

Objectives

1. The student will learn that the Web contains mostly current information.
2. The student will learn that web seraches are huge and time consuming in comparison to searches done in the online catalog.
3. The student will learn that no one search using any one seach engine will provide the necessary needed information.

I. What is the topic of your research project?

a. Translate your topic into a question.

Digitized and Non-Digitized Environments 111

    b.   Translate your question into controlled vocabulary (identity the proper vocabulary) for your topic.

II. Using the university's online catalog, identify resources in the library on your topic, using the terminology you established in Ib.

    a.   How many resources did you identify?
    b.   How many titles area available for checkout?
    c.   What is the location on campus of each item?
    d.   How many titles have a missing status?
    e.   How many of these titles are already checked out?
    f.   Check OhioLINK (a union catalog for approximately fifty libraries in Ohio) for availability of missing or checked out items, and request to borrow them.

III. Using the online catalog, identify indexes to search that would be appropriate for your topic.

    a.   Make a printout of each title containing the call number and location.
    b.   Retrieve the indexes you have identified and search for articles using the terminology you identified in Ib.
        1.   Select citations.
        2.   Search for the journal titles to see if this library has it in its collection.
        3.   Check to see that the library has the year you need of that journal.
        4.   Check to identify the location of the periodicals you need.

IV. Using excite as a search engine (http://www.excite.com) to locate information on your topic on the WWW.

    a.   What terminology did you use?
    b.   What was the format of your search?
    c.   How many hits did you retrieve?
    d.   Examine each hit and select the ones most appropriate for your topic and record the url for each selected.
    e.   Did each selected site provide you with a date?

V. Using Altavista as a search engine (http://www.altavista.com):
Answer the same 5 questions as in IV.

VI. Using Yahoo as a search engine (http://www.yahoo.com):
Answer the same 5 questions as in IV and V.

VII. Comparison of WWW searches:

a. Did you get the same results with each search engine?
b. Did you find the same materials with each one?
c. Were any of the searches you selected copyrighted?
d. Were you able to verify who was responsible for the sites you selected?
e. Did you receive any requests to pay fees for any of the materials you located?
f. What types of material did you find? (Full-text? Books? Articles? Bibliographies?)

NOTES

1. *Statistical Abstract of the United States.* Washington, DC: Department of Commerce, Bureau of the Census, 1997.
2. Network Wizard, *Internet Domain Survey.* http://www.nw.com.
3. Daniel J. Barrett, *Netresearch: Finding Information Online.* Sebastopol, CA: Songline Studios : O'Reilly & Associates, 1997.
4. Judith M. Pask and Carl E. Snow, "Undergraduate Instruction and the Internet." *Library Trends* 44 (Fall 1995): 306-317.
5. Daniel J. Barrett, *Netresearch: Finding Information Online,* 1997.
6. Marsha Tate and Jan Alexander, "Teaching Critical Evaluation Skills for World Wide Web Resources." *Computers in Libraries* 16 (November/December 1996): 49-52, 54-55.
7. Marydee Porter Ojala, "Hole in the Net and Its Web." *Searcher: The Magazine for Database Professionals* 5 (January 1997): 32-34, 36-37.
8. Mary Ann Fitzgerald, "Misinformation on the Internet: Applying Evaluation Skills to Online Information." *Emergency Librarian* 24 (January/February 1997): 9-14.
9. Walt Crawford and Michael Gorman, *Future Libraries: Dreams, Madness, and Reality.* Chicago, IL: American Library Association, 1995.
10. Cerise Oberman, "Library Instruction: Concepts and Pedagogy in the Electronic Environment." *RQ* 35 (Spring 1996): 315-323.
11. John O'Neill, "On Surfing–and Steering the Net." *Educational Leadership* 54 (January 1, 1996): 12-17.
12. John O'Neill, *Ibid.*, 15.
13. David Rothenberg, "How the Web Destroys the Quality of Students Research Papers." *The Chronicle of Higher Education* 43 (August 15, 1997): A4.

14. Walt Crawford and Michael Gorman, *Future Libraries: Dreams, Madness and Reality.* Chicago, IL : American Library Association, 1995.

15. Gertrude Himmelfarb, "Revolution in the Library." *American Scholar* 46 (Spring 1997): 197-204.

USING TABLOID LITERATURE TO TEACH CRITICAL READING SKILLS IN THE INTERNET ERA

Dan Ream

ABSTRACT

Even after being taught how to locate information for their research needs, many students lack the skills necessary to discern reliable, authoritative sources from those which are not. As the Internet and book superstores, such as Barnes & Noble, more frequently replace libraries as the places used to find information, researchers leave behind the protection of the carefully selected book and journal collection. Thus critical evaluation skills have grown even more important. By using sensational, often inaccurate articles from national weekly tabloids sold at supermarkets and newsstands, librarians can teach the criteria for evaluating information sources in a way that students find entertaining. Evaluation criteria revealed by use of tabloid examples include: authority of author and experts cited; attribution of sources; and misuse of language.

BACKGROUND

In 1984 the University of Tennessee Undergraduate Library, in collaboration with that campus's ALA-accredited library school, began offering a quarter-long credit course entitled "Finding Information: Resources and Strategies." Given the luxury of ten weekly meetings with the same students, it was decided early on to include sessions and assignments focusing upon critical reading and thinking skills necessary for students to evaluate information sources they might use throughout their lives. A lecture/discussion, assignment, and outside readings were prepared; copies of which are available on file from the LOEX Clearinghouse at Eastern Michigan University, as are materials from a 1989 presentation at the LOEX annual conference about the use of tabloids in teaching critical reading skills.

THE NEED

Information seekers are growing increasingly independent of libraries in their acquisition of information. In part, this may be explained by the media's realization that information presented in an entertaining way (or "infotainment") can draw a large audience. In television this phenomenon can be observed in the success of such programs as "Oprah", "Jerry Springer", "Hard Copy", "Dateline", "20/20", and "A Current Affair." In print, the products of this phenomenon include *People* magazine and a number of tabloid publications, such as the *National Examiner*, *National Enquirer*, and the *Weekly World News*. Readership of these publications far exceeds mainstream news publications such as *Newsweek*, *Time*, or *U.S. News & World Report*, as well as any scholarly journal.

More dramatically, the World Wide Web and access to full-text databases reduce the local control of libraries and librarians over access to information. No longer can students rest assured that they are drawing from a collection of sources shaped by librarian and/or faculty selector expertise and discretion. As students pick their own sources from the Internet and elsewhere, our instruction must teach them the critical skills necessary to evaluate the sources they find and use.

USING TABLOIDS AS A TEACHING TOOL

Holding up a tabloid newspaper in front of a group of college students invariably gets their attention: some students laugh, others smile, others roll their eyes, but all show their attention, which is not always a given in library skills instruction sessions. Asking a class if they have read one of these publications also gets a variety of reactions from embarrassment to wisecracks, but all college students seem to realize that supermarket tabloids enjoy a reputation for ridiculousness. This feeling of superiority to tabloids seems to boost students' confidence about discussing them in a critical way.

Figure 1.

As tabloid articles in both print and Internet form tend to be ephemeral, and few libraries hold back issues of these, the articles used as examples here should be regarded as illustrations only. Their exact citations were lost long ago. Suffice it to say the two articles used here are from the *National Examiner* in 1983 or 1984. Like-minded articles can be found on any newsstand or grocery store checkout line, and current ones may better reflect the anxieties or fantasies of the day.

Students were first given copies of an article entitled "Buffalo Bill Was Not A Wild West Living Legend." The article's approach can best be summarized by its opening sentence: "Legendary western tough guy Buffalo Bill Cody was in reality a mincing swish totally undeserving of his he-man reputation." After taking a few minutes to read the article, students were then asked if they believed the article to be accurate and why or why not. Through discussion, students usually come to notice these points: no author's name appears; no sources are quoted or attributed; the language used (such as mincing swish") is sensational; and the article's contents don't support the thesis. The process of discovering these evaluation points is described as "internal evaluation," meaning evaluation based solely upon the examining the article source itself.

Students were next asked how they would verify the accuracy of this story and they usually conclude that a search for other sources about Buffalo Bill should achieve this. They are then given an article from the *Reader's Encyclopedia of the American West*[1] to contrast with the previous article. In so doing, they find an author (with relevant credentials), sources that are attributed, and more objective/judicious use of language. Although he is here described as a "Showman", there is no inkling in this second source that Buffalo Bill was effeminate or a "mincing swish."

The use of language in news reporting is next discussed using the imaginary headline "27 Million Turkeys Murdered in North Carolina Massacre." This was the size of the previous year's turkey "harvest" in that state. Students were asked to brainstorm on how else this headline might be worded. A variety of possibilities are usually offered with disagreements as to the connotations of various suggested words. Students are then given a photocopy of the "to kill" entry from the *Webster's New Dictionary of Synonyms*[2] which explains the sometimes subtle differences in meanings between synonyms. Unlike most thesauri which serve as mere memory-joggers, this dictionary explains the differences

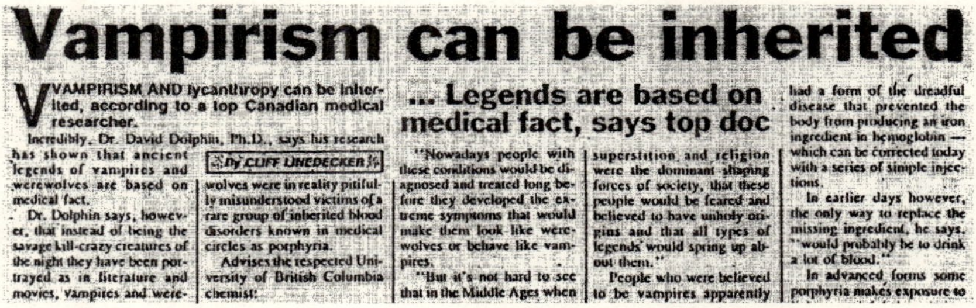

Vampirism can be inherited

VAMPIRISM AND lycanthropy can be inherited, according to a top Canadian medical researcher.

Incredibly, Dr. David Dolphin, Ph.D., says his research has shown that ancient legends of vampires and werewolves are based on medical fact.

Dr. Dolphin says, however, that instead of being the savage kill-crazy creatures of the night they have been portrayed as in literature and movies, vampires and were-wolves were in reality pitifully misunderstood victims of a rare group of inherited blood disorders known in medical circles as porphyria.

Advises the respected University of British Columbia chemist:

... Legends are based on medical fact, says top doc

"Nowadays people with these conditions would be diagnosed and treated long before they developed the extreme symptoms that would make them look like werewolves or behave like vampires.

"But it's not hard to see that in the Middle Ages when superstition and religion were the dominant shaping forces of society, that these people would be feared and believed to have unholy origins and that all types of legends would spring up about them."

People who were believed to be vampires apparently had a form of the dreadful disease that prevented the body from producing an iron ingredient in hemoglobin — which can be corrected today with a series of simple injections.

In earlier days however, the only way to replace the missing ingredient, he says, "would probably be to drink a lot of blood."

In advanced forms some porphyria makes exposure to

Figure 2.

in the meanings of synonyms. As such, it's a handy tool for studying word choice and connotations.

The use of language in tabloid publications for its shock value also warrants discussion, as attention-getting techniques are likewise on the mind of every headline writer and cover designer—even in the more traditional and mainstream press.

"Vampirism Can Be Inherited" is our next article for review and students are asked to critique this article also. Though the language remains "colorful," this article does show an author's byline, quotes a possibly reliable source, and the text does seem to support its own thesis.

Discussion shifts next to methods of "external evaluation," which is explained as being the use of other sources to verify the authority or accuracy of an article. Students were asked to look at biographical sketches of the expert quoted in the story (in *American Men & Women of Science*[3]) and the author who wrote the piece (in *Contemporary Authors*[4]). They note that the quoted expert has worked on the subject of the story, the blood disease known as porphyria. The author of the piece has also worked on related article topics as well, though he is a journalist rather than a subject expert. A medical dictionary definition is provided which shows that the disease does cause the symptoms as described in the article, such as sensitivity to light, receding gums, sensitivity to garlic, that sound similar to attributes given to human vampires.

Keywords for searching additional articles are next identified, with "porphyria", "vampirism" and "lycanthropy" (the study of werewolves) usually chosen. Two articles located through such a search are then shared. Last of all, a *Newsweek* article[5] on the same subject and quoting the same researcher is shown to the class. This article appeared several months after the tabloid article they have been examining. In essence then, this tabloid article on vampirism is substantially accurate, despite its use of tabloid lingo, like "top doc says." Finding accuracy, in this case then, is usually a surprise to those who automatically dismiss tabloid publications.

At this point the class has covered a variety of methods of internal and external evaluation of an information source. Lest they should think that such review is only called for when reading tabloid articles, the students are next presented with the case of Linus Pauling and his infamous 1970 book, *Vitamin C and the Common Cold*.[6] Anyone seeking biographical information on Pauling would be easily impressed by his many degrees and awards, which include two Nobel Prizes. Nonetheless, a literature search of that time period shows that Pauling's book on Vitamin C was the subject of great controversy in both scientific and popular journals.

In conclusion, students were warned to be skeptical, even of experts. On this subject, students were given an outside reading assignment of an essay by Richard Feynman entitled "Most Experts Don't Know More Than the Average Person."[7] Ironically, if we are to regard Feynman himself as an expert, we would be led to disregard his article!

Other sources for external evaluation are incorporated into the class's homework assignment; these include: finding and reading book reviews; reading letters to the editor following journal, magazine, or newspaper articles, biographical reference sources for finding expert and author credentials; and Katz's *Magazines for Libraries*[8] for noting journal bias.

THE INTERNET ERA

The World Wide Web, on which everyone is a publisher, offers a great deal of new fodder for teaching critical reading skills. Unfortunately, just like the print tabloids, web sites of this type are ephemeral and may disappear at any time. Nonetheless, here are a few sites that serve this purpose in the late 1990s.

The Weekly World News Internet Edition

http://www.wwnonline.com/
Like its print counterpart, the Internet edition is full of "interesting" stories for critical examination, such as "Bat Boy," the half-human, half-bat creature captured in a West Virginia cave. As in the story described above from a decade earlier, vampires are very popular on this web site, with stories such as "Is Santa Claus a Vampire?"

Feline Reactions To Bearded Men

http://www.improb.com/airchives/cat.html
The satirical journal the *Annals of Improbable Research* features this article in its online archive. It bears all the landmarks of a scholarly article, with footnoting statistical analysis, and so on, but when one discovers pseudo-sources like this:

> Seuss, Doctor, "Feline Responses to Hats," *Veterinary Developmental Studies*, July 1955, vol. 32, no. 7, pp. 5462 the joke is apparent.

The Alan Sokal *Social Text* affair

http://www.physics.nyu.edu/faculty/sokal/
Alan Sokal, Professor of Physics at New York University, submitted an article entitled "Transgressing the Boundaries: Toward a Transformative Hermeneutics of Quantum Gravity" to the scholarly journal *Social Text*, which published it, unaware that it was a joke, with language and concepts made up by the author. The article, and the furor that followed it can be read at Sokal's own web site.

The Onion

http://www.theonion.com/
The Onion does a good job of looking like a real newspaper with its humorous, though occasionally tasteless, parodies of top news stories, such as "ACLU Defends Nazis' Right To Burn Down ACLU Headquarters" or "Nike To Cease Manufacturing Products: 'From Now On, We'll Focus On Just Making Ads,' Says CEO."

Given these and other like-minded Internet sites, librarians have a multitude of options for tabloid teaching materials in the years to come.

NOTES

1. *Reader's Encyclopedia of the American West.* New York: Crowell, 1977.
2. *Webster's New Dictionary of Synonyms: A Dictionary of Discriminated Synonyms with Antonyms and Analogous and Contrasted Words.* Springfield, MA: Merriam, 1973.
3. *American Men and Women of Science: Physical and Biological Sciences* (14th ed.). New York: Bowker, 1979.
4. *Contemporary Authors: A Bio-bibliographical Guide to Current Writers in Fiction, General Non-fiction, Poetry, Journalism, Drama, Motion Pictures, Television, and Other Fields.* Detroit: Gale Research Co., 1981.
5. Seligmann, Jean. AVampire Diagnosis: Real Sick.@ Newsweek (June 10, 1985), p. 72.
6. Pauling, Linus. *Vitamin C and the Common Cold.* San Francisco: W. H. Freeman, 1970.
7. Feynman, Richard. "Most Experts Don't Know More Than the Average Person." *U.S. News and World Report* 98 (March 18, 1985), pp. 79-80.
8. Katz, William. *Magazines for Libraries.* New York: Bowker, 1969.

Is the information current?

TEACHING WEB EVALUATION
MEETING THE CHALLENGE

Marsha Ann Tate and Jan Alexander

ABSTRACT

The tremendous disparity in the quality of Web resources has presented a critical instructional challenge for teachers and librarians. This chapter addresses this challenge through the adaptation of traditional print evaluation criteria to accommodate the unique characteristics of Web-based communication. The chapter describes various evaluation techniques and curriculum materials that can be used to help instruct students how to evaluate the relative quality of Web resources. In addition, a variety of implementation strategies are also discussed.

INTRODUCTION

Web users share a common dilemma. On one hand, the Web offers access to a vast amount of information. On the other hand, these resources are a chaotic mixture of almost every type and quality of information imaginable. A major challenge librarians and other educators face in this Web-oriented environment is how to help users acquire evaluation skills so they can decide which Web resources are of value to them. In response to this dilemma, we have created a curriculum designed to help teach students how to evaluate Web resources. This chapter describes the three components of the curriculum, and how they work together. It also illustrates various ways we have implemented the curriculum at Widener University.

AN OVERVIEW OF THE CURRICULUM

The curriculum was developed for use with both undergraduate and graduate students at Widener. One of our main objectives was to incorporate flexibility into the curriculum so the materials could be tailored to the needs of individual classes. The curriculum was designed to be easy to understand, but not oversimplified. It was also designed to be practical. And perhaps most importantly, the curriculum was designed not to be dogmatic. We did not want to become arbiters of what is a "good" or "bad" Web page. Rather, we wanted to help students develop the skills they need to make their own judgements about what Web resources are valuable to them.

The curriculum materials, which are available at our Web site (Alexander & Tate, 1996-1999), include the following:

1. A PowerPoint presentation. The PowerPoint presentation describes:
- five traditional criteria used to evaluate print resources
- how to apply these five criteria to the evaluation of Web resources
- additional considerations which, because of the unique nature of the Web, need to be considered when evaluating Web resources
2. Five Evaluation Checklists. The checklists are composed of a series of questions that Web users can ask themselves when evaluating five different types of Web pages (advocacy, business/marketing, informational, news, and personal pages).
3. Actual Web Page Examples. When we teach the curriculum, we also show actual Web page examples that illustrate the various concepts described in the PowerPoint presentation.

CONCEPTS COVERED BY THE POWERPOINT PRESENTATION

Five Traditional Evaluation Criteria

The PowerPoint presentation defines five traditional print evaluation criteria (authority, accuracy, objectivity, currency, and coverage) and explains how these criteria can be adapted to the evaluation of Web resources.

1. Authority: "The extent to which information is the work of a person or organization recognized as having definitive knowledge of a given subject area" (Alexander and Tate, 1999). Analyzing the credentials of an author and/or publisher can often help determine the authority of print sources. However, on the Web, works are often self-published, and authors frequently neglect to list their qualifications for writing about the topic.
2. Accuracy: "The extent to which information presented is reliable and free from errors" (Alexander and Tate, 1999). The accuracy of many print sources is monitored by the presence of editors and fact checkers, and, in the case of scholarly works, by the peer review process. On the Web, however, much material has not been reviewed by editors or fact checkers, and the author may even fail to proofread the material before it is made public.
3. Objectivity: "The extent to which a document expresses facts or information without distortion by personal feelings or other biases" (Alexander and Tate, 1999). Traditionally, it was often quite costly for individuals or small groups to convey their views on an issue to a large segment of the public via print or broadcast media. The Web, however, has become a "virtual soapbox" for individuals and organizations that previously lacked a public forum for their ideas. It can sometimes be quite difficult to verify the sources of information on the Web, and to identify how the biases of the information provider might affect the objectivity of the information presented.
4. Currency: "The extent to which material can be identified as up to date" (Alexander and Tate, 1999). There are standards for many print materials that enable users to evaluate its currency. For example, most print materials include publication

and copyright dates. The Web, because it is such a new medium, does not have similar standards. As a result, many of the materials placed on the Web fail to include a publication or copyright date. And, if a date is present, it may not be clear to the user whether the date indicates when the material was first written, when it was first placed on the server, or when it was last revised.
5. Coverage: "The range of topics included in the work, the depth to which those topics are addressed, and the intended audience for the material" (Alexander and Tate, 1999). The coverage of a print source can often be determined from the introduction, table of contents, or index to the material. Because these features are absent in many Web sources, it can sometimes be difficult to ascertain the coverage of the material.

ADDITIONAL EVALUATION CONSIDERATIONS

Because of the unique nature of Web resources, the evaluation curriculum also emphasizes several additional considerations important to Web evaluation

Blending of Information, Advertising, and Entertainment

In print sources, there is often a clear visual distinction between the advertising and informational content. Likewise, radio and television commercials are also usually clearly differentiated from the programming content. On the Web, however, these distinctions are often far less obvious. As a result, many Web pages blend information and advertising to such a degree that it can be difficult to differentiate between them. The PowerPoint presentation cautions users to be aware of this fact, and encourage them to analyze the source of both the informational and advertising content of the page. We also stress the need to be aware of the potential influence of advertisers and sponsors on the objectivity of the information. Moreover, if entertainment is offered on the page, we encourage students to question why the entertainment is provided. If the entertainment serves as an enticement to purchase a product or service, users need to be aware of this.

Challenges Presented by Frames, Hypertext Links and Search Engines

Frames, hypertext links, and search engines are Web innovations that can significantly impact the evaluation process. A user may access one Web page that provides authoritative and reliable information, and assume that any pages linked to it are also from authoritative, reliable sources. Unfortunately, because of the nature of hypertext links, this may not always be the case. Similarly, on a page that includes frames, it may not be evident to the user that the information in the various frames may be coming from different sources. Therefore, we stress the need to evaluate, not only each Web page, but also the contents of each frame, independently.

In addition, search engines can retrieve individual Web pages out of the context of the Web site in which they reside. Unless a page retrieved in this manner includes information concerning who is responsible for the page, or provides a link to this information, a user may not be able to determine the accuracy and authority of the information on that page.

Additional Challenges

The PowerPoint presentation also cautions users to be aware that:

- requirements for additional software may limit access to certain information on the page
- Web pages can be altered, either deliberately or accidentally
- Web pages are inherently more unstable than print, and therefore the user may not be able to access the page again at a later date.

WEB PAGE EXAMPLES

An important part of our classes, in addition to providing a theoretical background in how to evaluate Web resources, is the presentation of actual Web page examples that illustrate the various concepts presented. These examples include not only illustrations of the traditional evaluation criteria of authority, accuracy, objectivity, currency and coverage, but also examples of the additional evaluation challenges unique to the Web.

We usually discuss the criteria of authority, accuracy and objectivity together, as they are frequently so intertwined. To illustrate these criteria, we show a page from "The Smoker's Home Page" Web site (http://www.tezcat.com/~smokers/). This site includes a page entitled "Essays on the Anti-Smoking Movement" (http://www.tezcat.com/~smokers/issues1.html) by someone named Joe Dawson. We discuss how to determine the authority, accuracy, and bias of the information presented on this page. For example, we begin by showing that, although an email address is given for Joe Dawson, no further information about Mr. Dawson or his qualifications for writing on the topic are provided. We also point out the lack of adequate reference information to support the statistics about smoking that are included in the essay. Moreover, we talk about the possible reasons that the site was created, and how this might affect the objectivity of the information provided.

To illustrate the concepts of currency and coverage, we show two pages from the ARTFL Project's Web site, *Roget's Thesaurus* (http://humanities.uchicago.edu/forms_unrest/ROGET.html) and *Webster's Revised Unabridged Dictionary, 1913 Edition* (http://humanities.uchicago.edu/forms_unrest/webster.form.html). Both of these pages demonstrate the need, not only to pay attention to the date the material was first written, but also to explore what revisions may have been made to the original work.

To illustrate the blending of advertising, information, and entertainment, we show a site such as the Nabisco *Chips Ahoy* Web site (http://www.chipsahoy.com). This site's pages have a colorful, bright blue background with giant chocolate chip cookies floating tantalizingly down the left-hand side of each page. The site's eclectic offerings present games for children and curriculum materials for teachers, all interspersed with the omnipresent cookies.

IDENTIFYING SIX TYPES OF PAGES

We have discovered that, because Web pages contain quite different types of information, there is no "one size fits all" way of evaluating them. Therefore, we have identified five categories of Web pages, each of which requires a separate evaluation checklist. (The pages in our sixth category, entertainment pages, have as their primary purpose to provide enjoyment, so for our purposes we did not create a formal evaluation checklist.)

For our evaluation procedure, we have identified the following six types of pages:

1. Advocacy pages. Advocacy pages promote a cause or an idea.
2. Business/marketing pages. Business/marketing pages promote a product or service.
3. Informational pages. Informational pages provide statistical or research information, or a schedule of events.
4. News pages. News pages provide current information, whether it is national, international, or local.
5. Personal pages. Personal pages present a personal expression of something—often an idea, an artwork, or a hobby, for example.
6. Entertainment pages. Entertainment pages encompass a wide variety of topics, including games, jokes, parody, and so forth.

For each of these categories, we have created a checklist of questions a user can ask to help determine:

- the relative information quality of the page
- whether the page will be of value to them or not

THE CURRICULUM'S THREE STEP EVALUATION PROCEDURE

Once a student understands the theoretical underpinnings of Web resource evaluation, we move to the curriculum's next phase: a practical application of the concepts. The transition from theory to practice involves the following three-step evaluation procedure:

Step 1: Determine the type of page to be evaluated
Step 2: Select the appropriate checklist for that type of page
Step 3: Apply the checklist questions to the page to determine the information quality of the page and whether the page will be useful to you or not.

USE OF THE CURRICULUM AT WIDENER UNIVERSITY

Because the amount of time we have available for teaching faculty and students varies widely, we attempted to make the materials flexible so they could be used either in parts or in their entirety.

Use of the Materials in Their Entirety

The following examples illustrate ways Widener librarians have presented the curriculum materials in their entirety:

- Faculty Development Programs. Faculty development programs offer an excellent opportunity to "get the word out" to faculty about the curriculum. During these sessions, we also demonstrate how Web evaluation techniques can be integrated into a wide range of disciplines. We have discovered that once faculty members were made aware of the materials, a number of them subsequently adapted the materials for use in their classes, independent of our involvement.
- Library Instruction Sessions. Although Widener University does not offer a formal for-credit library research course, a number of faculty members set aside one or more of their class periods during the semester for formal library instruction. Not surprisingly, Web evaluation has been one of the more popular library instruction requests in the past few years. As a result, the sessions afford us the opportunity to teach both undergraduate and graduate students in disciplines as diverse as economics, education, hospitality, and nursing. Graduate education students have found the materials particularly helpful, since many of them also face the challenge of applying these concepts in their work with K-12 students.

Use of Selected Components of the Curriculum

We have successfully integrated selected portions of the curriculum into a variety of teaching situations. These situations usually arise when time constraints prevent use of all the available materials or when a faculty member requests we present specific portions of the curriculum.

The following examples illustrate instances when we have used portions of the materials rather than the entire curriculum:

- Undergraduate English 101 Library Instruction Classes. Widener University's undergraduate English 101 classes normally require librarians to cover a multitude of topics in a single 50-minute class session. Adding another topic to this already full agenda at first seemed impossible. However, we discovered that we could readily incorporate a number of Web evaluation concepts into the classes on an informal basis. For example, as we taught students how to use Web search engines, we discuss the information quality of the pages retrieved.
- Undergraduate and Graduate Library Instruction Classes in Other Disciplines. Another popular library instruction request from both undergraduate and graduate faculty is to teach students how to locate and evaluate Web resources in specific subject areas. In these instances, we often show the PowerPoint presentation in its entirely, but substitute Web page examples relevant to the subject matter of the class being taught for the more "generic" ones we normally use.
- Nursing Library Instruction Classes. The librarian who works with the nursing students was asked to present classes on evaluating Web medical-related resources. She created an effective curriculum that included showing a portion of the PowerPoint presentation, as well as providing a list of Web resources specific to the field of nursing. She also made copies of the PowerPoint slides to hand out to the students, to enable them to have a printed copy of the evaluation ideas she had presented.
- Undergraduate Hospitality Library Instruction Classes. In another instance, the students in an undergraduate Hospitality class were asked to find Web resources about a variety of people important to the hospitality industry. A search for Web sites on Howard Hughes, for example, turned up numerous resources, some reliable and useful, others of dubious quality. The class discussed how much they could trust the biographical information about Howard Hughes found on these various Web sites.
- Graduate Education Instruction Classes. In yet another class, graduate education students were required to design a portfolio for a specific math-related topic. They were required to locate

activities and lesson plans on the Web relating to their topic and to use the concepts in the PowerPoint presentation to evaluate these resources.
- One-on-one Work with Individual Students. In addition to using the Web evaluation materials in our formal library instruction classes, we also find them useful as we assist students on an individual basis at the reference desk. We often find ourselves referring to the concepts included in our curriculum materials as we teach students, not just how and when to use the Web, but how to use it wisely.

The tools and techniques described in this chapter have arisen out of our current Web evaluation needs. As Web technology changes and as Web content grows ever more sophisticated, we continue to face new evaluation challenges. As a result, there will be an ongoing need to adapt existing Web evaluation methods to this constantly changing Web environment.

REFERENCES

Alexander, J., & Tate, M.A. (1996-1999). Evaluating Web Resources [Online]. Available: http://www.widener.edu/libraries.html (Select *Evaluating Web Resources*) [1998, February].

Alexander, J., & Tate, M.A. (1999). *Web Wisdom: How to Evaluate and Create Information Quality on the Web*. Mahwah, NJ: Lawrence Erlbaum Associates, Inc.

Chips Ahoy (1998). [The Chips Ahoy Web site]. [Online]. Available: /http://www.chipsahoy.com [1998, February].

"Essays on the Anti-Smoking Movement" (1994-95). [The Smoker's Home Page" Web site]. [Online]. Available: (http://www.tezcat.com/~smokers/issues1.html) [1998, February].

Roget's Thesaurus. [The ARTFL Project Web site]. [Online]. Available: (http://humanities.uchicago.edu/forms_unrest/ROGET.html) [1998, February]

[The Smoker's Home Page Web site] (1997). [Online]. Available: (http://www.tezcat.com/~smokers/) [1998, February].

Webster's Revised Unabridged Dictionary, 1913 Edition. [The ARTFL Project Web site]. [Online]. Available: (http://humanities.uchicago.edu/forms_unrest/webster.form.html) [1998, February].

Copyright held by Marsha Ann Tate and Jan Alexander.

EXERCISES

NAME THAT COUNTRY!
A MAP EXERCISE AS AN INTRODUCTION TO THE LIBRARY REFERENCE COLLECTION

Izabella Tomljanovich

OBJECTIVES

This exercise is led by a librarian and designed for college freshmen as a part of their initial orientation to the library, and specifically the reference collection. It is most effective if the assignment is endorsed by the course instructor and then graded. It may be used for a wide variety of courses, as long as they deal with geographical information. Its aim is multifold:

- Teaching the students about a particular geographical area and its features;
- Instructing them in the use of the library catalog;
- Orienting them to the organization of the library;
- Familiarizing them with select reference tools; and
- Teaching them how to evaluate the chosen map or atlas.

PROCEDURE

The library session is divided into two equal parts, first is the mechanics of locating sources and the second part is using these sources critically. The following is a suggested breakdown of activities. They will differ depending on your library and its collections.

Locating Sources:

- Introduce students to library policies, layout, classification and catalog;
- Provide various examples of searches for reference materials using the catalog;
- Point out any special locations for regular and oversized atlases and maps.

Using Maps and Atlases:

Allow students to gather atlases they have identified with the help of the catalog. Using one atlas as an example, explain the basis for evaluation of a reference tool:

- authority: publisher, author
- publication date
- scope
- audience
- map characteristics: type, scales, projection, index, color, font, symbols, and so on

Ask students to examine their chosen atlas for a short period of time paying attention to the front and back matter: the title page, its verso, table of contents, introduction, bibliography, index, and so forth.

Pass out the map assignment to be completed individually after class. Provide a map outline of the appropriate region and time period and ask students to identify countries, main cities, bodies of water, and so on. The extent of detail the students need to fill in will vary.

It may include, for example, a series of map outlines for the same region at different time periods. The assignment then may demand the identification of time periods as well. (A copy of a collection map outlines can be found in the American Map Company's School Series).

EXPERIENCE WITH THIS EXERCISE

This exercise has proven highly effective for a freshman seminar dealing with the last two centuries of literature and culture in Eastern European countries. Implemented in the beginning of the semester, it provided the students with a basic and required understanding of the region and its complex history reflected in its ever-changing borders.

Since students often ignore publication dates, the library session started a discussion of present-day borders. Most of the atlases required the students were using were out-of-date but it took a while for the students to realize that. The assignment required the students to identify countries at different times in the nineteenth and twentieth centuries and cite which reference work they used. The course instructor corrected the map assignment and gave the students a copy of a properly done exercise. She referred to that exercise, as well as other maps and atlases throughout the course.

In addition to the various print resources, *Centennia*, a CD-ROM produced by Clockwork Software (1994) proved to be a great visual help. The program is a guide to the history of Europe and the Middle East from the year A.D.1000 to 1994. It is composed of very detailed, dynamically evolving maps which can be zoomed to different scales. Also, the maps are accompanied by short descriptions, and both graphic and texts can be searched by historical names, places, and dates.

SIFTING DOWN TO THE GOLD: TEACHING STUDENTS TO CRITICALLY EXAMINE WEB SITES

Julie Bockenstedt

Many librarians face the challenge, as we demonstrate the mechanics of searching myriad electronic resources, of also teaching students how to recognize quality information on the Internet where resources of varying value appear side-by-side. We are all familiar with the traditional criteria for evaluating sources: the author's qualifications, currency of the material, the point of view (bias or slant), and so on. All of these points can be made and duly recorded by the students, but a hands-on, specific example teaches students strategies for *how* to do this. My object was to create a simple, yet elegant assignment that gives students direct and meaningful contact with assessing information on the Internet.

As psychology liaison, I was invited to conduct a session on Internet sites related to psychology and, more specifically, help students locate information on the topic of college student binge-drinking. This lesson grew out of a seemingly serendipitous, but actually frequent event while exploring resources on the Net. I did a sample search on HotBot for statistics on this topic and was lead to a "golden" page,[1] one that any student looking for statistics in this area would love to find. However, the page had no indication of the author, the currency of the statistics, nor the source(s) of these statistics. From this I created an assignment that gives students "what they want," but also requires them to prove that it is worth their interest.

OBJECTIVE

Most of us who have used the World Wide Web, whether skeptically or not, have found the golden nugget, that perfect piece of information. This *does* happen. The problem arises when students do not distinguish between the excellent and the dubious. Many students, no matter how sophisticated they may have become with search engines, print off the nugget and consider their research complete without examining the who, what, and why of this information. The Web site I use for this exercise is perfect since key information is not evident on the page located by the search engine. Search engines often find pages linked off of a main page. Even if the site creator has the credentials and regularly updates the site, the pages buried two, three or more layers deep often do not contain that vital information.

I would suggest when implementing this exercise that you use a "golden" or "fool's gold" site for the topic or discipline on which the students are working. It does not matter if this site contains valid or invalid information: the important thing is to find a page that does not have in evidence the author or currency of the information. In fact, if there is enough time, students could examine an example from both ends of the quality spectrum. The object is to have the students get comfortable with navigating through a Web site and locating markers of quality.

PROCEDURE

When doing this exercise, I give the students a print-out of the site and show them the search that found the information. After the students have time to appreciate such "perfect" information, I tell them they cannot use it in their paper until they evaluate it. Then I give them a step-by-step guide to follow.

Who

The first task the students learn to do is decompose the different elements of a URL in order to find who has posted this information on the Web. I have them identify the domain address that will lead to the home page of the creator. I also have them guess who the creator might be before they move back to the home page. Many do not realize what .edu, .gov, .com, and so forth, signify. By teaching them this with reference to the URL in hand, the students start to appreciate the origin of the information. In this particular case, the URL is a commercial site, and I have the students tell me what they expect when they arrive at the home page. The students then delete the separate components of the URL, starting from the back, until they reach the domain address. In my particular example, the students have to back up two pages before the home page.

Once the students arrive at the home page, I have them write down the author as well as any other pieces of information they can glean about the organization/person/college. Do they recognize the name? Is there any way of discovering the reputation of the provider from the page? Are there any clues from the graphics or composition of the page about the intent of the provider? I also indicate that a librarian or professor would be willing to help them answer these questions.

When

The initial statistics page also does not include the date the site was created, updated, nor the currency of the statistics themselves. I have the students explore the opening page to see if they can find any indication of when the site was created. Then I have them explore the links that lead them forward to the initial page with the statistics.

What and Why

As the students explore the currency question, I also have them seek out the original source of the statistics, since it appears that the creator of the page is not the producer of the statistics. As they follow the links to the initial page they discover bibliographies for the different pages of facts as well as the funding source of the page. The bibliographies provide an opportunity for a second-level of evaluation, by having the students copy down a few of the citations to pursue and assess.

WHERE DO THEY GO FROM HERE?

One last step in the research process can be pursued if there is time. I suggest to students that they try to find comparable statistics from other sources (preferably covered in instruction) and contrast the two sets of statistics. However, just navigating through the site is pivotal in getting them started in the evaluation process. Many of the students when first confronted with the task of finding out who, what, when, and why think it is a daunting task. The steps in this exercise, by requiring them to ask pertinent questions, give them the beginning skills for investigating the source of information.

The library has traditionally held evaluated material for patrons. Even though we are starting to select excellent Internet resources for our students, we have to address the assumptions and difficulties they have when choosing Internet sites on their own. This is especially important today since professors are increasingly using the Web in class and students are often starting their research on the Web.

NOTE

1. "Facts and Statistics." Available: http://www.glness.com/ndhs/stats.html

TZMHR2
THE ANDERER EYE TEST

Natasha Cooper

"Which is better?" Eye doctors ask this question as they show us blurry and clear letters on a screen during an eye examination. The Anderer Eye Test was developed so that librarians might also ask the question "which is better?" in an attempt to encourage students at the college level to consider which of many possible information resources is best for their particular assignment.

The Anderer Eye Test is named for Tammy Anderer, Visiting Instructor of Nursing at Lycoming College, in whose class it was first used. The Lycoming College Nursing Department as a whole places emphasis on use of recently published scholarly literature and therefore introductory nursing courses (such as those taught by Ms. Anderer) are appropriate places in which to introduce the idea of careful examination of search results.

The test is primarily a vehicle to convey an idea at the start of a library instruction session. It consists of a simple overhead transparency with the large letters T Z M H R 2 on it. It can be shown out of focus or in focus with a mere twist of the knob, accompanied by the question: "which is better?" This question is crucial at a time when students, many of whom have access to a wealth of search services and indexes, may be flooded with search results. Students need to learn how to sift through these results and select the most promising. They need to ask "which is better?" or "which are likely to be most useful to me?"

How do students sift? What makes some results seem better than others? Students appear to use a variety of methods to select. Among others, they may choose citations based on number of pages (sometimes shorter is preferred to longer as opposed to the other way around), appropriateness of title, availability in library (or even better, on the computer monitor), and possibly whether or not any results are available at all on a system with which the student is familiar (in other words, a student may select a database/service/index with which the student is already comfortable over a potentially more appropriate but less familiar database/service/index).

The Anderer Eye Test was designed to initiate discussion about sifting and selecting. After showing blurry and clear images of the eye chart letters, the librarian describes a specific topic and shows the class selected citations related to that topic. The librarian asks the students which citations are better (sometimes the librarian asks the students to decide which they would try to borrow through Interlibrary Loan, if unavailable in the library). The librarian may add that there are no right or wrong answers.

The citations usually include one from a scholarly journal paired with one from a newspaper. Other variables include page length; date of publication; whether there is a bibliography; appropriateness (or existence) of descriptors or subject headings; publisher (if any—government personal web page, and so on); language; type of document (dissertation, scientific report, book, chapter, brochure), and so forth.

Students typically react by commenting first on the subject. They will say "the first one seems to be more closely related to the topic." Prompts from the librarian can point out differences in whatever variables seem appropriate. After several pairs, the students start to pick up on other clues, noting years of publication, language, and other factors.

This exercise opens the door for discussion. It provides the opportunity to talk about types of publications and the publishing process. If the students are attending with their faculty member as part of a regularly scheduled class, the faculty member should be invited to comment as well, which usually results in further discussion. The librarian can sometimes bring other topics into the discussion in a natural way, such as how students start the Interlibrary Loan process.

Some of the citations have obvious variations (for example, three citations about the topic of stress might come from a peer-reviewed medical journal, a linguistics publication and an engineering publication). Other variations are more subtle—both articles may be related to the topic, but in only one citation does the topic appear as a subject heading. The examples aren't always paired. The librarian has sometimes used one and simply asked what its good and bad points are. Some examples are fun. For example, one biology class compared citations about bats and the final citation was about head trauma incidents following bat day at Yankee Stadium. Such examples, of course, can lead to a discussion about careful selection of search terms. The librarian may also encourage the class to examine types of resources, for example, a page from a printed index, a page of citations with abstracts, an online indexing service, or personal web page with (or without) a bibliography.

These citations may be shown as overhead transparencies on a screen or projected directly from an on-line service. The librarian may use web pages as samples or prepare a web page with links to citations for consideration. The librarian may use a written form of this exercise in worksheets, providing several citations and asking whether the student would fill out an interlibrary loan request for each item.

DISADVANTAGES AND ADVANTAGES OF THE APPROACH

- Superficial? One implication of the exercise is that students can dismiss entire articles by merely looking at a citation. Students do need to be encouraged to actually look at a few articles in their entirety (even if it means leaving the computer to walk to a different floor!) while conducting their research. The idea of perseverance can be mentioned in the session.
- Faculty involvement required. As with most library instruction sessions, this exercise works best with the support of the faculty involved. If faculty are not concerned about the types of materials cited in papers turned into them, this exercise is less fruitful!
- Student or librarian? The exercise comes dangerously close to implying that students need to think like librarians. Just because a student's selections from a list of search results are not the same as those of a librarian does not mean they are necessarily poor

choices. The emphasis has to be on the appropriateness for that person for that project.
- Differences in skimming habits. The exercise doesn't analyze differences in skimming practices. Do librarians skim and select differently because they do it more frequently and are better able to decipher the baffling elements of a citation than students are? Is this simply a question of increased practice or are there other elements in the learning process that enable users to evaluate search results or index entries (and if so, what are these)? The exercise does not have a strong theoretical basis, although it does support development theories such as those of Perry (1970), as students move from a clear polarity (right or wrong) to more complex or contextual relativity.
- Who is best suited to evaluate? In a discussion on the BI-L listserv, Stehle (1998) questioned whether it is the librarians' role to evaluate resources or whether this is more rightly the role of the subject specialist (professor) or student using the material. In a setting where librarians are generalists (as may be the case in a small academic library), librarians' abilities to evaluate results in subject areas may be limited. The librarian needs to remind students that for this particular part of the session, the emphasis is on looking at structural clues in citations as opposed to subject matter, although subject is important too during the whole process (and may be covered by the professor in other parts of the session or course).
- Searching skills. Stehle (1998) also observes that teaching searching skills and database selection are important aspects of instruction (perhaps more important than evaluation). While this exercise does not focus on database selection or searching techniques, the latter can be included if the librarian talks a bit about search terms and subject headings. This exercise is also flexible enough that it can take five minutes of a session or 30, leaving time available to be devoted to database selection and other issues.
- Easy to prepare. This exercise can easily be presented with overhead transparencies, live on the Internet, with presentation software or it can be used in a written format. Students don't seem to get too glassy-eyed as long as they are being asked to scrutinize the citations and talk about what they see.

- Flexibility. The exercise may be used with a large or small class. It can be varied by subject or may focus on particular areas of a library's collection. It can be varied in length and easily changed at the last minute, or even mid-session, depending on the nature of the discussion.

The main strength, however, is that it opens the door for discussion and is a start at addressing the ever-important need for evaluation and an accompanying concept, selection. As students see more and more web pages, vast and vaster on-line services, and possibly a few print indexes, they need to learn how to evaluate and select. Helping them do this is a challenge for librarians.

APPENDIX

Sample Written Version of the Exercise

Assume that the following citations are for articles related to your topic (even if they are not really related to your actual topic). Indicate whether or not you would request the following articles using the library's Interlibrary Loan/Document Delivery service.

TI: The good news about diabetes
AU: Vinicor-F
AA: Centers for Disease Control and Prevention, Atlanta
SO: Bottom-Line Health (BOTTOM-LINE-HEALTH) 1997 Jan; 11(1): 9-11
SB: Consumer-Health (H); USA (US)
PY: 1997
DE: *Diabetes-Mellitus-Therapy
DE: Diabetes-Mellitus-Drug-Therapy; Diabetes-Mellitus-Insulin-Dependent; Diabetes-Mellitus-Non-Insulin-Dependent
SH: Therapy-; Drug-Therapy
DT: journal
LA: English
SN: 1092-0129
UD: 9706
AN: 1997020026

_____ This would be a good article to request (top priority). (Why?)
_____ This is a good article, but wouldn't be my first choice. (Why?)
_____ I wouldn't bother to get this. (Why?)

* * * *

TI: Life-change events model in analyzing diabetic patient's blood glucose and body weight control [Chinese]
AU: Liang-CA; Boehm-S
SO: Nursing-Research (China) (NURS-RES-CHINA) 1995 Dec; 3(4): 298-308 (30 ref)
SB: Nursing (N)
PY: 1995
DE: *Diabetes-Mellitus-Non-Insulin-Dependent; *Models-Theoretical; *Life-Change-Events; *Body-Weight; *Blood-Glucose
DE: LISREL-; Factor-Analysis; Michigan-; Age-Factors; Sex-Factors; Socioeconomic-Factors; United-States; Male-; Female-
DT: journal; research; tables-charts
LA: Chinese
UD: 9704
AN: 1997014541
XFLD: AB; RF

_____ This would be a good article to request (top priority). (Why?)
_____ This is a good article, but wouldn't be my first choice. (Why?)
_____ I wouldn't bother to get this. (Why?)

* * * *

TI: Confidentially. Diabetic emergency: forgotten snack
SO: Nursing (NURSING) 1996 Apr; 26(4): 21
SI: N34580000
SB: Core-Nursing (C); Nursing (N); USA (US); Peer-Reviewed (P)
PY: 1996
DE: *Diabetes-Mellitus-Complications; *Diabetic-Coma-Etiology
DE: Middle-Age; Inpatients-; Female-
SH: Complications-; Etiology-

DT: journal; anecdote; brief-item
LA: English
SN: 0360-4039
UD: 9605
AN: 1996016154

_____ This would be a good article to request (top priority). (Why?)
_____ This is a good article, but wouldn't be my first choice. (Why?)
_____ I wouldn't bother to get this. (Why?)

* * * *

TI: Social support and knowledge level of the older adult homebound person with diabetes
AU: Zink-MR
SO: Public-Health-Nursing (PUBLIC-HEALTH-NURS) 1996 Aug; 13(4): 253-62 (29 ref)
SI: SR0050967
SB: Core-Nursing (C); Nursing (N); USA (US); Peer-Reviewed (P)
PY: 1996
DE: *Support-Psychosocial-Evaluation-In-Old-Age;
 *Homebound-Patients-In-Old-Age;
 *Risk-Assessment-Psychosocial-Factors;
 *Health-Knowledge-Evaluation-In-Old-Age;
 *Home-Health-Care-In-Old-Age;
 *Diabetic-Patients-In-Old-Age
DE: Funding-Source; Connecticut-; Pilot-Studies;
 Research-Instruments; Reliability-; Content-Validity;
 Clinical-Assessment-Tools; Purposive-Sample;
 Nonexperimental-Studies; Descriptive-Research;
 Norbeck-Social-Support-Questionnaire;
 Diabetes-Mellitus-Insulin-Dependent-In-Old-Age;
 Aged-; Aged-80-and-Over; Outpatients-; Male-; Female-;
 Diabetes-Mellitus-Non-Insulin-Dependent-In-Old-Age;
 Questionnaires-; Record-Review; Home-Health-Agencies
SH: Evaluation-; In-Old-Age; Psychosocial-Factors
IN: Home Care Social Support Assessment Guide; Homebound Diabetes Knowledge Level Questionnaire; Diabetes Clinical Indicator Tool

GR: Partially funded through a Connecticut State University research grant give to Dr. Zink
DT: journal; questionnaire; research; tables-charts
LA: English
SN: 0737-1209
UD: 9703
AN: 1997011681
XFLD: AB; RF

_____ This would be a good article to request (top priority). (Why?)
_____ This is a good article, but wouldn't be my first choice. (Why?)
_____ I wouldn't bother to get this. (Why?)

* * * *

TI: Self-regulation: negotiating treatment regimens in insulin-dependent diabetes
AU: Jayne-RL
SO: UNIVERSITY OF CALIFORNIA, SAN FRANCISCO 1993 PH.D. (243 p)
PY: 1993
DE: *Diabetes-Mellitus-Insulin-Dependent; *Diabetes-Mellitus-Insulin-Dependent-Psychosocial-Factors; *Patient-Compliance; *Self-Regulation; *Diabetic-Patients; *Decision-Making-Patient
DE: Pearson's-Correlation-Coefficient; Multimethod-Studies; Visual-Analog-Scaling; Semi-Structured-Interview; Grounded-Theory; Convenience-Sample; Hemoglobins-; Male-; Female-
SH: Psychosocial-Factors
DT: dissertation; abstract; research
LA: English
UD: 9604
AN: 1996009358
ON: UMI Order #PUZ9322264
XFLD: AB

_____ This would be a good article to request (top priority). (Why?)
_____ This is a good article, but wouldn't be my first choice. (Why?)
_____ I wouldn't bother to get this. (Why?)

Citations reprinted from CINAHL databases with permission.

REFERENCES

Perry, William G., Jr. 1970. *Forms of Intellectual and Ethical Development in the College Years: A Scheme.* New York: Holt, Rinehart and Winston, Inc.

Stehle, Douglas M. 1998. "Re: Summary: Teaching 'Facts' & 'Opinions'." In BI-L (Digest 13 Feb 1998 to 16 Feb 1998) [listserv]. Binghamton, N.Y. [cited 17 February 1998]. Available from bi-l@bingvmb.cc.binghamton.edu.

PANNING FOR GOLD:
EVALUATION THROUGH PROCESS RESEARCH APPROACH

Sheryl Nisly-Nagele and Soo Lee

Students are faced with many class assignments for which they are required to produce some information. Often having some information, regardless of the quality, satisfies the assignment. Yet it is obvious to most users of information that there are differing qualities of information for any information need. In an attempt to help students learn how to retrieve and use the best available information for a research question, a project was designed to sharpen their research and critical thinking skills in a carefully developed process research approach.

The setting for the project is a physiological psychology course designed to be one of the earlier courses in the major. The course has an overall philosophical theme, the mind/body issue. After an introduction to this theme, most of the rest of the semester is devoted to the work of learning physiological psychology per se. About two-thirds of the semester is used to introduce basic principles related to this discipline. The last one-third is devoted to student presentations on a topic of interest that is both intricately related to physiological psychology, but that also addresses the mind/body issue (tied to their research project). Their final exam is a paper in which each student synthesizes the material from a number of student presentations and, based on their individual synthesis of the material, articulates their position on the mind/body issue. The interdisciplinary nature of the course material lends itself to the project requirement of a topic that is addressed both in the biological and psychological literatures.

Preparation for the presentation is a semester-long research project that is divided into several steps. Students are given feedback after each step and are required to have the instructor sign off on each part before going to the next part. The directives for each step are included in the workbook (available upon request from the authors), as are spaces for them to write, as necessary. Also included are evaluation sheets for the instructor, and a place for the instructor's sign-offs.

The process research approach includes the following steps for students to complete: (1) formulate a research question using secondary reading on the topic and taking notes on the reading (The question must be approved by the instructor.); (2) develop search strategies; implement searches using both biology and psychology databases (PsycLIT and Medline) to access the primary literature and refine the searches until they yield a literature that tightly addresses the research question (no more than 20-25 citations); (3) select the most useful research reports from the database searches and retrieve the reports; (4) evaluate the retrieved reports for their relevance to the research topic by highlighting the relevant parts; (5) prepare multiple drafts of an outline and a presentation of findings on the research question in the class (10-15 minute oral presentation).

The success of the project is embedded in: (1) frequent intervention by the instructor at each step of the research process before students are allowed to go to the next step. The steps that require the most feedback and intervention occur while students are completing the database searching for their research question and are doing the first draft of their presentation; (2) close collaboration with the instructor and the liaison librarian who provide instruction and assistance in the database searching process and the use of proper controlled vocabulary. Since many of the students have been exposed to basic database searching, the emphasis of the project and of the instruction is on using controlled vocabulary. Even students who have considerable experience using databases to access research often require intervention before they understand how to refine a search so that they have the most relevant material related to their topic; (3) complete integration of the research project into the curriculum. Since the project focuses on issues central to the course, and the presentations are the basis for the final, the project has a great deal of relevance for the students. Students take on the project with both excitement and seriousness since they know that other students will rely on them for the information needed for the final paper. Furthermore, since the project content is so intimately tied to the course content, the material students are encountering in their projects often naturally come up for class discussion.

More often than not, the first try does not yield an effective search. Limitations of the search are noted by the instructor, and the student is required to redo the search. Suggested search terms are often included in the feedback. In many cases, a second try yields a successful search, but sometimes additional searches are required. If a student still has not honed in on a usable search after two tries, the student usually is asked to work with the instructor in person so that more interactive direction can be given. Now that the databases are readily accessible from the instructor's office, it is quite convenient to work with students directly on the database, helping them to complete successful searches in the instructor's presence.

The most difficult aspect of the process for students to grasp is the usefulness of controlled vocabulary. Most students are accustomed to doing keyword or free-word searches. Often the best way to communicate the usefulness of controlled vocabulary is to use it with the searcher who has tried unsuccessfully to get to the heart of the research literature using free-word searches. Someone who has been unsuccessful using one approach is often ripe for suggestions about another workable approach!

The attached computer printout—including a search history along with instructor's feedback—illustrates the process described above.

STUDENT THESIS: DEPRESSION IS A MAJOR PREDICTOR OF SUICIDE

PsycLIT Search #1

#	122436	DEPRESSION
#	24091	SUICIDE
#	31134	DEPRESSION and SUICIDE

TI: Clinical measures of rapid onset of action.

AB: Discusses definitions of early onset of action and presents evidence that supports an early onset with currently available antidepressants, including venlafaxine. The benefits of an antidepressant with an early or rapid onset of action include a more rapid resolution of the debilitating symptoms of depression, a potential reduction in the risk of suicide and cost savings associated with a reduction in hospitalization. While these benefits are valuable, this promise has yet to be fulfilled by any antidepressant. Venlafaxine is a unique serotonin-noradrenaline reuptake inhibitor which produces rapid and prolonged desensitization of beta-adrenergic receptors in preclinical studies after both acute and chronic administration of venlafaxine. Results from placebo-controlled and active comparator clinical studies provide evidence that venlafaxine may have an early onset of activity which is most apparent at higher dosages, and thus may fill the long awaited need for an antidepressant with an early onset of action. (PsycLIT Database Copyright 1997 American Psychological Assn, all rights reserved)

DE: ANTIDEPRESSANT-DRUGS; DRUG-THERAPY; PSYCHOPHARMACOLOGY-

TI: Correlates of suicidal behavior in a juvenile detention population.

AB: The present study identifies the correlates of current suicidal ideation and past suicide attempts among 555 adolescents in a county juvenile detention center. All Ss completed a questionnaire. Suicidal behavior in delinquent boys was generally associated with depression and decreased social connection, whereas suicidal behavior in delinquent girls was associated with impulsivity and instability. Current ideation was most significantly associated with current depression. In multivariate analyses, past attempts were associated with suicidal ideation and ineffective coping for males, with major life events and impulsivity for females, and with not residing with at least 1 biological parent prior to detention for both males and females. (PsycLIT Database Copyright 1997 American Psychological Assn, all rights reserved)

DE: ATTEMPTED-SUICIDE; PERSONALITY-CORRELATES; SUICIDAL-IDEATION; ADOLESCENCE-; JUVENILE-DELINQUENCY; REFORMATORIES-
TI: Patients' reactions to the suicide of a psychotherapist.
AB: This descriptive exploratory study examines the behavioral and affective reactions of clients to the suicide of their psychotherapist 1 year after the event, including remembered responses upon first hearing of the suicide. 12 19-49 yr old Ss completed questionnaires. Initial grief reactions of Ss were found to be similar to other suicide survivors with strong attachments to the deceased, including depression, numbness, anger, hopelessness, and panic. One yr after the event, several Ss continued to discuss the event with friends, had persistent feelings of depression and abandonment, and continued to deny the death as a suicide. A reluctance to reenter therapy was also reported. Almost all Ss stated that suicide was an acceptable solution to some problems. These results suggest the potential existence of pathological grief for many Ss in this study. Implications for the mental health community and intervention services for patient survivors are discussed. (PsycLIT Database Copyright 1997 American Psychological Assn, all rights reserved)
DE: CLIENT-ATTITUDES; PSYCHOTHERAPISTS-; SUICIDE-; ADULTHOOD-; IMPAIRED-PROFESSIONALS

Instructor's feedback: Note that this search yielded over 1,000 references. This means that the search is very broad. Since the search needs to be narrowed by topic (not by year or journal), the best way to narrow it is to determine what subject headings are used to access the literature for your topic. When a free-word search is used, as in this search, any citation that includes the searched term is retrieved, even if the term is one of the author's names! In the first three citations retrieved, the first and third citations don't address the issue of how good a predictor depression is for suicide. The second citation may slightly address this issue. Please redo the search by using the Thesaurus to locate the appropriate subject headings. When you enter the term you are interested in, the Thesaurus should help you determine the appropriate subject headings.

PsycLIT Search #2

- # 121062 MAJOR
- # 222436 DEPRESSION
- # 34091 SUICIDE
- # 4370 (MAJOR DEPRESSION IN DE) AND (SUICIDE IN DE)

TI: Prediction of suicide intent in Aboriginal and non-Aboriginal adolescent inpatients: A research note.

AB: The relationship among depressive symptoms, anxiety, hopelessness, and suicidal intent was explored in a group of 77 adolescents who had been hospitalized after attempting suicide. Data were collected for the study by retrospective review of patient records. Regression analyses indicated that hopelessness was the only significant predictor of suicide intent in Caucasian Ss, and depressed mood was the only significant predictor in the Aboriginal group. Clinicians should be aware that measures of hopelessness may be of limited value in assessing suicidal risk in Aboriginal adolescents. (PsycLIT Database Copyright 1997 American Psychological Assn, all rights reserved)

DE: ANXIETY-; HOPELESSNESS-; MAJOR-DEPRESSION; SUICIDE-; ADOLESCENCE-; WHITES-

TI: More on melatonin.

AB: Describes a female (aged 14 yrs) with a history of depression, sexual abuse, substance abuse, and one suicide attempt who took an overdose of melatonin. Effects of the overdose included blurry vision, drowsiness, dizziness, and confusion. The S was oriented to person, place, and time, and her vital signs were stable. Results of a physical examination were within normal limits with the exception of the neurological findings. The S exhibited slow beats of lateral nystagmus, a finding which has not previously been documented in melatonin ingestion. S was treated with activated charcoal and released from a psychiatric unit after 9 days. The nystagmus had resolved by the time she was seen on the psychiatric unit. (PsycLIT Database Copyright 1997 American Psychological Assn, all rights reserved)

DE: DRUG-OVERDOSES; MELATONIN-; NYSTAGMUS-;
      ADOLESCENCE-; CASE-REPORT; DRUG-ABUSE;
      MAJOR-DEPRESSION; SEXUAL-ABUSE;
      SIDE-EFFECTS-DRUG; SUICIDE-
TI: Hospitalizing the suicidal adolescent: Decision-making criteria of psychiatric residents.
AB: Investigated the criteria used by general psychiatric residents in determining the appropriateness of hospitalization. A questionnaire containing 64 vignettes describing adolescent suicide attempts was completed by a sample of 33 residents from a general psychiatry training program. Six variables known to relate to lethality of attempt were systematically varied within the vignettes (gender, depression, conduct disorder/substance abuse, previous attempts, suicidal relative, and family supports). Ss were asked to judge the appropriateness of hospitalization for each vignette. Results show that hospitalization preference was significantly predicted by all risk factors except for gender, with the presence of depression emerging as the most important predictor of hospitalization. Residents recommended hospitalization more frequently than did experienced child and adolescent clinicians. In comparison with experienced clinicians, residents placed more importance on depression, and less importance on conduct disorder/substance abuse, in making decisions to hospitalize. Although psychiatric residents use known risk factors for adolescent suicide in assessing hospitalization need, there was clear support for further training initiatives for this population. (PsycLIT Database Copyright 1997 American Psychological Assn, all rights reserved)
DE: CLIENT-CHARACTERISTICS;
      CLINICAL-JUDGMENT-NOT-DIAGNOSIS;
      PSYCHIATRIC-HOSPITALIZATION;
      PSYCHIATRIC-TRAINING; SUICIDE-;
      ADULTHOOD-; ATTEMPTED-SUICIDE;
      CONDUCT-DISORDER; DRUG-ABUSE;
      FAMILY-RELATIONS; HUMAN-SEX-DIFFERENCES;
      MAJOR-DEPRESSION; MEDICAL-RESIDENCY

Instructor's feedback: This search is certainly more narrowed than the previous one! The search is still retrieving many more citations than can be handled successfully in a 10-15 minute presentation, however. (Remember, the recommended maximum number of citations is 20-25.) At this point, consider what subtopic you might be interested in focusing on; this probably will be the most effective way to narrow the search now. As I look at the citations included here, I see several more focused topics you might want to consider: You could narrow the topic to a particular population, like adolescents. Or, you might want to look at attempted suicide in particular, rather than suicide which is carried out. Or, you might want to focus on how drug abuse factors in with depression to effect suicide. Please spend more time reviewing these citations and use them to help you further focus your interests.

PsycLIT Search #3

#	121062	MAJOR
#	222436	DEPRESSION
#	34091	SUICIDE
#	412323	ADOLESCENTS
#	511	(MAJOR DEPRESSION IN DE) AND (SUICIDE IN DE) AND (ADOLESCENTS IN DE)

TI: Diagnostic comorbidity of mental disorders among young suicides.

AB: Depressive and substance use disorders predominate in the psychopathological backgrounds of suicides of all ages. In 5 published studies of consecutive suicides by adolescents and young adults, the average reported rates are 41% for major depression and 48% for substance abuse. Personality disorders (PDs) have been less consistently reported with rates varying from 10 to 34% among young suicides. These consist almost exclusively of borderline and antisocial personality disorders. "Pure" PDs are rare because of comorbidity with major depression and substance abuse. Follow-up studies of patients with PDs also report similar comorbidity among those who die by suicide. Hypothetical explanations are given for this observed comorbidity. (PsycLIT Database Copyright 1993 American Psychological Assn, all rights reserved)

DE: COMORBIDITY-; SUICIDE-; MAJOR-DEPRESSION; DRUG-ABUSE; PERSONALITY-DISORDERS; ADOLESCENTS-; YOUNG-ADULTS

TI: Modern psychiatric views of adolescent depression and suicidal behavior. Special Issue: Adolescent depression.
AB: Reviews adolescent depression in terms of prevalence, diagnostic measures used, etiology, types of depression, and treatment. Adolescent suicide is discussed and the possibility of organic factors is addressed. Practical consequences of biological differences in suicide have not yet been adequately explored. The importance of balancing medical with counseling interventions is emphasized. (PsycLIT Database Copyright 1991 American Psychological Assn, all rights reserved)
DE: MAJOR-DEPRESSION; DIAGNOSIS-; ETIOLOGY-; TREATMENT-; SUICIDE-; ADOLESCENTS-
TI: The current age of youthful melancholia: Evidence for increase in depression among adolescents and young adults.
AB: (This reprinted article originally appeared in the *British Journal of Psychiatry*, 1988 (Jan.), Vol. 152, 4-14. The following abstract of the original article appeared in PA, Vol. 76:5252.) Discusses the rise in rates of depression among adolescents and young adults, particularly the increase in suicide attempts and death. Data from large-sample family studies and community epidemiological surveys are reviewed and reanalyzed, using life-table statistical methodology. Evidence for secular trends is presented, and the problems of disentangling period and cohort effect are discussed. It appears that the population born in the years after World War II have had increased rates of depression and other related illnesses, including drug abuse and alcoholism. Theoretical implications are discussed, particularly for gene-environment interactions. (PsycLIT Database Copyright 1991 American Psychological Assn, all rights reserved)
DE: MAJOR-DEPRESSION; EPIDEMIOLOGY-; SUICIDE-; SOCIAL-CHANGE; CHILDREN-; ADOLESCENTS-; YOUNG-ADULTS

Instructor's feedback: It looks like you are home free! You have a modest number of citations all of which address the same issue. Your hard work has paid off! Now, as you read the articles, you still may find that the thesis needs to be modified to fit your research; that is fine. Research is a dynamic process, so the readings will shape the thesis just as much as the thesis will determine how and what is read. Get back to me if you want further help. Good work!

LIFE AND DEATH MATTER:
INFORMATION EVALUATION FOR NURSING IN THE REAL WORLD

Sandra Jamison and Soo Lee

The Messiah College Nursing Department has been very intentional about helping students develop information literacy skills which they will need to be effective in a rapidly changing, information-driven profession. A coordinated plan for giving students instruction in and experience with various dimensions of information literacy has been developed jointly by the nursing liaison librarian and the faculty of the Nursing Department over the last five years. Although information literacy goals for students have remained unchanged, learning experiences and instructional methods have been improved subsequent to assessment by students and faculty.

There are many different assignments throughout the four years, but one project in the final semester demonstrates the integration of all previous experiences with an emphasis on evaluation of the information and the information search process. This project gives students experience in asking questions, locating, obtaining, evaluating, and integrating the information needed to address a variety of situations that they might face in the first two years of practice.

Eight problem situations are given to six groups, each with seven to eight students. Each group must work on two of the eight problem situations (listed below). Near the end of the semester, each group reports to the class and submits a folder of documentation for each situation worked on. To successfully complete the project students must:

1. Identify what information they need or might consider to solve the problem.
2. Identify possible sources of that information.
3. Retrieve the information from pamphlets, experts, web sites, databases, audiovisual material, newspapers, and so forth.
4. Evaluate the quality and content of various pieces of information including a consideration of their source. (See Information Evaluation Checklist developed for this assignment.)
5. Evaluate and describe their information search process and collate all the information including an evaluation of each source.
6. Integrate the information gathered into a classroom presentation.

The first year the assignment was used, students were not given any particular format to use in evaluating information. The liaison librarian did give a one-hour presentation with accompanying handouts on assessing the value of different types of information. The products students submitted clearly lacked the evaluative dimension. They simply collected information and wrote a one-to-two-page summary of the process of obtaining materials and findings. There was no evidence of evaluation of sources.

The second year, the assignment was refined. An Information Evaluation Checklist was developed collaboratively by the liaison librarian and the course instructor Students were asked to submit a completed checklist for each source used. More students were assigned to respond to each problem situation, and each group was asked to present its findings to the class, explaining how various information sources were evaluated.

Students' responses to the assignment the second year indicated a more sophisticated understanding of the evaluative dimension of information literacy, but the assignment needs additional refinement and more specific teaching on the critical elements of information evaluation. The results, though inconsistent, were much improved over those of the first year. Information Evaluation Checklists were completed for many of the sources. It was not evident, however, that students had incorporated the concept of relative value of different sources in synthesizing responses to the problem situations. The next time the assignment is given, it will be important to spend more classroom time teaching students how to use evaluation of the information in arriving at a solution. Time, the complexity of locating material, and the intricacies of group dynamics for seniors excited about graduating, likely influence the effectiveness of learning from the assignment described. A suggestion for others considering such an exercise would be to include it earlier in the curriculum.

Following is an example of one situation and a summary of the work submitted by three students:

You have been offered an entry-level position by two different hospitals. Both positions look equally attractive when you compare most of their attributes. They offer comparable hours, opportunities, benefits, and so forth. Both would be within commuting distance for you. There is one difference between them, however, and you wonder how it might impact your working experience there. In one hospital, individual contracts are negotiated directly with the hospital, whereas in the other hospital, the State Nurses' Association is the collective bargaining agent and the nurses working there are represented as a bargaining unit in contract arrangements. What are the implications of being (or not being) represented by the State Nurses' Association in contract negotiations—both positive and negative? As you weigh the various implications, keep in mind that as the health care revolution continues, mergers among hospitals are a frequent occurrence.

In response to the situation described, three students (Esselburn, Risley, Sundheim) gathered information from a variety of sources and evaluated each source using the Information Evaluation Checklist. Their sources included:

A newspaper article on a group of nurses considering joining a union
A letter from hospital management to nurses considering unionization
Information from two Internet sites: a national professional organization with collective bargaining activities and a home page of one of the State Nurses' Associations very active in collective bargaining
Several articles from professional nursing journals, one by a lawyer explaining a particular labor law
An editorial in a nursing journal
A chapter in a book on issues in nursing
Printed informational brochures from a State Nurses' Association

The "Initial Appraisal" sections of the Information Evaluation Checklists were complete and straightforward. The "Content Analysis" section write-ups demonstrated that students discriminated among the sources based on the source's objectivity, currency, and coverage. For example, students wrote that the lawyer's journal article "is factual and appears to be well researched." In contrast they said that the editorial was "opinion not substantiated by research. The author is definitely biased in his experience.... The view presented in this article does not extensively discuss all nurses' views but more importantly is an example of one individual's philosophy." They also said that the letter from hospital management was "Commercial/educational...information valid but author is somewhat biased against unions....Substantiates other material, primary in nature, marginally covers the topic." In evaluating the publications of the State Nurses' Association, the students wrote,

> The information that is presented is both fact and propaganda. It makes the organization sound so appealing and interesting that nurses would want to join it. Yet, at the same time, it is fact about what the Association does. I believe the author's point of view is biased and makes...[it] sound like the best organization to join because of its many great benefits ....This information stands by itself and adds new information. This material is primary because it comes from the organization itself.

The final page of material submitted listed the advantages and disadvantages of nurses participating in collective bargaining. In the class presentation students also gave their personal thoughts on union membership based on what they had learned.

The other seven problem situations and the Information Evaluation Checklist are included for additional information on this assignment which will be refined continually—both to teach and to assess nursing students' ability to achieve the college-wide information literacy goals.

SITUATION 1

You know that a responsibility of the professional nurse is to participate in professional organizations. Thus, you want to know the mission, membership requirements, and membership services of two types of professional organizations you are considering joining. Your task is to find the necessary information on each type of organization: (1) a specialized organization that would help you develop in your chosen area of nursing, and (2) one of the generalized nursing professional organizations.

SITUATION 2

One of your mother's best friends recently was given the option of several different treatment plans for breast cancer. During a complete mastectomy with removal of nodes, three nodes tested positive for cancer. Your mother asks you, as a nurse, to help her friend find information on the following:

> Most recent treatment options and their relative risks and benefits
> Current research for which her friend might be eligible
> Specialists in the management of breast cancer
> Support groups for her and her family

SITUATION 3

At the end of a staff meeting, one of the nurses on your unit mentions that she heard "guided imagery" and "reflexology" would soon be introduced as alternative nursing measures to promote relaxation and healing. In-services on the technique and practice of these measures will be required of all nurses on medical/surgical units in the next six months. You recall hearing about these alternative healing modalities on the Bill Moyer's TV special "Body and Mind" and want to learn more about them prior to attending the in-services. How would you proceed to gather information and to critique these two nursing measures and what questions would you want to have answered to participate in them?

SITUATION 4

Your church asked you to develop a display table of health resource information that would be relevant to members of the local community. Knowing there is a vast amount of information available—much more than you have time to gather or display—you want to know what topics will be of greatest relevance to people in your community. With this in mind, you need to gather information on age and gender of the population in your county, the leading causes of death by age group, statistics on marital status, employment and income, ethnic composition, and church membership. Gather this information for one county in any state.

SITUATION 5

As a recent graduate working in an inner city hospital, you have encountered many challenging questions and situations. Today, a patient with chronic renal failure, with whom you have built a trust relationship over the past week, confides that she is very concerned about her grandmother, an illegal immigrant who lives with her. Her grandmother has become increasingly weak in the past two months, has a productive cough and chest pain, and has experienced a 15-pound weight loss. She knows her grandmother needs help and may have an illness that could be transmitted to her two preschoolers. She asks you how to get health care for her grandmother without jeopardizing her position as an illegal immigrant.

SITUATION 6

The health care agency where you work recently announced there would be an "open enrollment" period of one month for all employees to sign up for one of three health plans offered as part of their benefits package. In order to make the best choice, you must compare what it would mean to have health care through Aetna, Inc., Travelers, or CIGNA. Decide what questions you need to ask and how to answer them. Then compare the relative advantages and disadvantages of the three health plans for your situation.

SITUATION 7

You are beginning to think about graduate school, even though you know it will be at least two years before you are ready to start. You want information on graduate programs in your field of specialization within your geographical area. What information would you need to gather, and from what resources?

INFORMATION EVALUATION CHECKLIST

I. INITIAL APPRAISAL
1. Author/Information Provider
   What are the author's credentials—educational background, past writings, and experience in this area?
   Is the information on a topic in the author's area of expertise?
2. Date of Publication
   When was the information published/created/updated/revised?
   Is the information current or out-of-date for your topic?
3. Nature of Information Source
   Is the information source commercial, educational, popular, scientific, other? This distinction is important because it indicates different levels of complexity and detail at which the subject is treated.
4. Publisher/Sponsor
   Is the publisher/sponsor reputable?
   What institution (company, government agency, university, other) or Internet provider supports this information?

II. CONTENT ANALYSIS
1. Intended Audience
   What type of audience is the author addressing?
   Is the publication (or information) aimed at a specialized or a general audience?
   Is the information too elementary, too technical, or just right for your needs?
2. Objectivity
   Is the information fact, opinion, or propaganda?
   Does the information appear to be valid and well-researched, or is it questionable and unsupported by evidence?
   Is the author's point of view objective and impartial? Or biased and partisan?
3. Coverage
   Does the information update other sources, substantiate other materials you have read, or add new information?
   Does it extensively or marginally cover your topic?
   Is the material primary or secondary in nature?

ABOUT THE EDITORS

Sue K. Norman spent her first adult career teaching remedial reading and writing at Wilbur Cross High School, New Haven, Connecticut. Her second career sees her as a librarian at the Waidner-Spahr Libraries, Dickinson College, Carlisle, Pennsylvania, where she has worked since 1980. At Dickinson, she has worked and administrated in almost every department of the library. She is serving her second term on the Instruction Committee for Diverse Populations, Association of College and Research Libraries, and has presented several poster sessions at ALA, including the one which led to this book. As instruction coordinator, she recognizes how essential it is to educate the campus in ways to evaluate materials found during the research process. Students, in particular, need to realize that they are the ultimate search engine.

Steven Vincent began his career as a reference librarian at Georgia State University, then served in various capacities, including head of reference and online services coordinator, at Dickinson College. In 1995, he joined the staff of Southern Polytechnic State University as head of reference. He co-teaches a section in the university's Science, Technology, and Society program entitled "Information, You and Society," for which his contributions include the history of information use and the evaluation of information.

ABOUT THE AUTHORS

Several of our contributors are already known for their work in teaching or advocating evaluation of Internet sources. Several of those we drew on for our poster session. A few came to our attention through their contributions to listserv discussion lists, such as BI-L. Others are colleagues we have worked with for a number of years.

Jan Alexander and *Marsha Ann Tate* are reference librarians at Widener University, Chester, Pennsylvania. Their interest in evaluating Web resources grows out of their work as instruction librarians. As they realized how much students were increasingly utilizing the Web in their research, they saw a great need to teach them how to evaluate the quality of the information they found. They maintain a Web page where their teaching materials may be found (http://www.widener.edu/libraries.html; select "Evaluating Web Resources"). They have recently expanded on their ideas in a forthcoming book, *Web Wisdom: How to Evaluate and Create Information Quality on the Web.*

Steve Black has been reference, instruction, and serials librarian at the College of Saint Rose in Albany, New York, since 1995. His current research interests emphasize evaluating the quality of journals (both print and online), and improving the library's methods of instruction. He looks at ways to determine the quality of information as a serials librarian, as an instructor to groups of students, and as a reference librarian. These synergistic perspectives have given him a broad perspective on the issue of information quality.

Julie Bockenstedt is a librarian at Dickinson College, Carlisle, Pennsylvania.

D. Scott Brandt is an Associate Professor of Library and Information Science at Purdue University. In his current position as Technology Training Librarian at Purdue his training reaches out to all levels at the university, from staff to faculty, and focuses primarily on concepts needed for learning in an information environment. He teaches a course called "Information Strategies" and his research centers on active teaching and constructivism in complex information environments. He presents workshops internationally on applying innovative techniques to training on Internet-related topics.

Doug Cook is media/reference librarian at Shippensburg University in Shippensburg, Pennsylvania. He teaches library instruction sessions as well as general instruction sessions about the World Wide Web. He presented a workshop at EDUCOM in Minneapolis in October 1997 entitled "World Wide Web Search Site Comparison," and he also helped plan and present a workshop for a Pennsylvania consortium on "Subject Directories and Search Engines." He looks on the Internet as being a monstrous encyclopedia in the sky. Although he is fascinated by the ease with which it is possible to find a bit of information about almost anything by searching the Web, he is concerned about learning how to tell the sheep from the goats.

Natasha Cooper is a references and education services librarian at George T. Harrell Library, Penn State College of Medicine, Hershey Medical Center, Hershey, PA. As a former instructional services librarian at Lycoming College in Williamsport, PA, she was also responsible for providing public services for the library's government documents collection. She is interested in information seeking habits of users of all ages and their abilities to identify what they are using. She says she is concerned about the number of hours we spend in front of computer screens.

About the Authors

Jennifer Dorner is an instruction librarian at Ball State University in Muncie, Indiana. Previously she has worked in the Science/Business/Social Sciences Department of the Memphis/Shelby County Public Library. She provides instruction to the campus community in which Internet searching and evaluation techniques play an ever-increasing role. Recognizing the vital need for health care professionals to use the Web wisely, she collaborated with a faculty member, Dr. Kay Hodson-Carlton, on a web-based instruction module entitled "Evaluating Health Care Information on the World Wide Web" for a graduate nursing class.

Carol Doyle is Information Services Training Coordinator for the University of California Santa Barbara Library as well as collection manager for Business/Economics and International documents. *Janet Martorana* is the Instruction Program Coordinator for the UCSB Library as well as the Environmental Sciences and California documents collection manager. They teach credit bearing classes on information research, as well as numerous one-shot classes. When they began teaching Internet use five years ago, they concentrated on teaching search techniques. However, they found that many students were indiscriminate in which information resources they selected. In the last few years, they changed the emphasis to the evaluation of information resources and over time have developed exercises and techniques that address how to evaluate resources.

Trudi E. Jacobson is the coordinator of user education programs at the University at Albany, SUNY, a position she has held since 1990. Prior to this she was Coordinator of Reference Services at Siena College, Loudonville, New York. Her principal areas of interest are critical thinking and active learning as applied to user education. She has presented workshops and published in these areas, as well as on user behaviors in connection with electronic resources. She and Laura B. Cohen recently published an article entitled "Teaching Students to Evaluate Internet Sites" in *The Teaching Professor* (July/August 1997).

Sandra Jamison is in the Nursing Department at Messiah College in Grantham, Pennsylvania.

Hal P. Kirkwood, Jr. is an Assistant Professor of Library and Information Science at Purdue University. He is currently coordinator of reference at the Management and Economics Library. He edits and authors a column in *Online* magazine called "Bookmark Central" that collects evaluated and annotated sites. He presented "Beyond Evaluation," a presentation at the 199 Online World Conference that recommended to librarians and information professionals the need for more collaboration in evaluating Internet resources.

Soo Lee recently retired from the Murray Library at Messiah College in Grantham, Pennsylvania.

Janet Martorana is the Instruction Program Coordinator for the University of California Santa Barbara Library as well as the Environmental Sciences and California documents collection manager.

Sheryl Nisly-Nagele formerly taught in the Behavioral Science Department of Messiah College in Grantham, Pennsylvania.

Dan Ream is head of Instruction and Outreach Services at the Virginia Commonwealth University Library in Richmond, Virginia. Formerly, he was head of reference at VCU and reference librarian at the University of Tennessee Undergraduate Library in Knoxville, Tennessee. In addition to teaching library and Internet research skills at VCU, he also teaches Internet research workshops for the CAPCON Library Consortium in Washington, DC, and the PALINET Library Network in Pennsylvania. He has done conference presentations at the LOEX Library Instruction conferences on promotion of library instruction and the use of tabloid literature to teach critical reading. He has also been a featured speaker at LOEX and several other conferences on the topic of "glitch management"—the prevention and management of technical failures while teaching or speaking in groups.

Bennie P. Robinson has worked in public, academic and medical libraries in Mississippi, New Jersey, Tennessee, and West Virginia, and is now at the University of Akron, Akron, Ohio. With the advent of the new millennium and the exploding access to global and instantaneous information, she, as an instruction librarian, is concerned about the lack of requirements for intellectual content.

About the Authors

Susan Taylor is instruction librarian in the Bracken Library, Ball State University, Muncie, Indiana. She began her career as a reference librarian at Ball State in 1993, moving to instruction in 1995, when the World Wide Web was beginning to make serious inroads into the library. Her concern about the quality of information students were finding on the Web inspired a presentation with a colleague, Dena Siegal, at the 1997 LOEX Conference on "Teaching Library Users to Evaluate WWW Resources." She also presented several sessions with another colleague, Melissa Muth, at the 1997-1999 Hypermedia Conferences in Muncie entitled "No More Hit or Miss: How to Effectively Search and Evaluate Web Resources."

Izabella Tomljanovich was formerly a librarian at Dickinson College, Carlisle, Pennsylvania. She is now working in The Hague, Netherlands.

Kappa Waugh is currently an instruction/reference librarian at Vassar College in Poughkeepsie, New York. Her parents, both academics who doodled and drew cartoons, reared her to think drawing was a reasonable way to take notes, remember things, pillory foolishness, and entertain herself and others.

INDEX

Alta Vista, 61
The Anderer Eye Test, 147

Blue Web'n, 67,68

Cataloging, to provide infrastructure and superstructure for information, 58, 60-61
Cenennia, 141
"Cereal syndrome", xiv-xv
Clinton, William, Technology Literacy Challenge, 6, 104
Collection management librarians
 missing from the WWW, 7
 not validating "subject authorities" on the WWW, 9
 traditional gatekeeping function, 19, 28-29, 31, 58, 61, 74, 117
 and web resources, 31
"Confusion factor" (*see* "Cereal syndrome")
"Cool," as evaluative concept for web sites, 66, 75
Crawford, Walt, 107
Criteria for evaluation, 11, 21, 63-64, 105-106
 author identity, 59, 77, 129
 clues of accuracy, 78, 129
 critical look at experts, 122
 currency, 77-78, 129-130, 141

holistic approach, 37
journal bias, 122
need for aesthetic sensibility, 24
not universal, 24, 29
statement of scope vs. mission statement, 76
worksheet example, 48-49
Critical thinking skills
 in library electronic resources instruction, xv,35
 obstacles to teaching by computers, xiv
 process-oriented approach, xvi, 157-158
 requirement for specific problems with web resources, 36-37, 122-123

Dublin Core project, 58, 60-61

Educational Resources Information Center (ERIC), 28
Electronic vs. print formats, x, 96-97
 advantages of print for accumulated knowledge, xii
 bypassing traditional gatekeepers, 18
 ease of download of Internet data, xiii

impermanency of information on the web, 26-27, 58, 105, 131
for periodicals, xiii
physical documents "self-incriminating," 58
timely information and the Internet, xii
Evaluation
   as an acquired skill, xiv, 17, 19-20, 30, 74, 84, 150
   and evaluating reviewers, 67
   "external," 121
   "internal," 120
   need for background knowledge, 18-19
   as a requirement of all information, xv, 12
   in scholarly disciplines, 56
   skills development process example, 168-169
   of web pages as a challenge for librarians, 62
   WWW source, 11, 21, 37
   (*see also* Criteria for evaluation; Evaluation exercises)
Evaluation exercises, 21-22, 39, 85, 148
   checklists for five categories of Web pages, 132-133
   comparing web and journal articles, 42-43
   decomposing URLs, 145
   identifying *site affiliation*, 40
   information checklist, 173-174
   link between *citing* and *evaluating*, 39-40
   map usage as library orientation device, 139-141
   showing *continuity between print and web resource evaluation*, 40-41
   three step procedure, 133
   use of tabloids, 117, 119
   using *domain*, 40

web tutorial for nursing students, 83-84
Faculty
   advanced skills in resource evaluation, 20, 30, 150
   involvement in library instruction, 134, 149
   view of students' research abilities, 29, 108
   views of Internet and research, xv, 82, 97, 109
Feynman, Richard, 122

GALILEO project (Georgia), x
Gatekeepers of information, 56
   and clashing frames of reference, 22-23
   (*see also* Collection management librarians; Publishers)
Gorman, Michael, 107
   updated five traditional laws of library service, ix-xi
Grey literature, 27, 75

Hahn, Susan E., annotated resource of evaluation of web information, 94-95
HotBot, 8
   and a "golden" page, 143

Information types
   "Infommercials," 79
   "Infotainment," 118
   no clear demarcation on the web, 36, 130
Internet Guide (Encyclopedia Britannica), 66-67

Kanzler, Joni, 37
Kwan, Julie, 37

Laws of library service, ix

past and future as complements update, xi
protect free access to knowledge update, x-xi
respect all formats of knowledge communication update, x
serve humanity update, x, xvi
use technology to enhance service update, x
Learning styles
  and library pathfinders, 109
  reader types and the Internet, xiii-xiv
Library
  demise predictions, xi
  and information scope vs. Internet, 108
  and recreational reading material, 31
Library instruction
  at Ball State University, 75-76, 79-84
  at Lycoming College, 147
  at Messiah College Nursing Department, 167, 170
  at the University at Albany, 92-93
  at University of California, Santa Barbara, 37-38
  at the University of Tennessee, 118
  at Widener University, 11, 128
  creation of demand for quality, 62
  in evaluative skills, 17, 104, 127
  "Johnny Appleseed approach", 45
  need for dynamic approach, xv
  need to teach best source vs. format, 6, 36
  "research skills of the new millennium," 4
  revolution, xiii-xvi
  team teaching benefits, xvi
  types, 38-39
Magazines for Libraries, 122
Magellan, 66, 75
Marr/Kirkwood Official Guide to Business School Webs, 67-68

Medical information on the Internet, concerns about quality, 83, 135
"MultiMedia Mediocrity" (MMM), 62

"Noise distraction," xiv

Oberman, Cerise, 107
Osler, Sir William, xiii

Pirsig, Robert, 25
Print formats (*see* Electronic vs. print formats)
Project Gutenberg, x, 107
Project Renaissance, 92-94
Publishers
  and peer review, 57, 106
  as safety net providers, 19, 27, 36, 74
  "vanity" presses, 57

Quality, 25-26
  and authentication via editorial or peer review, 61
  and authoritative source, 61
  and evaluation by subject specialists, 61
  need for both subjective and objective judgement, 26, 64-65, 130
  need for relative judgement also, 63
  unique characteristics of WWW resources, 26-27, 65, 130-132
Quality control (*see* Gatekeepers of information)
QuickTime, xii

Research
  appropriate tool selection, xv, 29, 47
  as a cyclical process, xvi
  and online resources, xiv
  as a teaching goal of librarians, xiii
  time commitment requirements, 19, 104, 149

(*see also* Search strategies; Tool analysis)
Rothenberg, David, 107-108

Search strategies
  and controlled vocabulary, 158, 159
  and instruction, 5, 7, 21, 43, 150
  and search engines, 8, 10, 61, 79, 131
  the "seduction factor" in Web data, xiv
Sokal, Alan, *Social Text* parody, 22-23, 24, 28-29, 123
"Spider" program type, 9
  and other automated retrieval programs, 61
Standards, cross platform multimedia, xii
Stoll, 107-108

Tate, M., and Alexander, J., 12, 37, 62, 94, 128
Technological revolutions, not instantaneous, xi
Tool analysis, xvi, 108

Web publishing
  costs, xii, 106
  drawbacks to authors, xi
  and scholarly articles, xiv
  as a vanity press, 60, 74
Webster's New Dictionary of Synonyms, 120-121
World Wide Web (WWW), 6-7
  characteristics beyond textual content, 26-27, 79, 118
  disparity in quality, 127
  free resources vs. computerized databases, 11, 20-21, 29, 43, 67, 118
  impedes student awareness of range of information sources, 94
  lack of formal structure, 59
  questionable sites, 80, 95-96
  six types of pages, 132-133
  size, 8, 27, 108
  as a soapbox, 10-11, 78
  as a way to bypass traditional gatekeepers, 18, 27
WWW Virtual Library, 29

Yahoo, 7-8, 61, 75

ZA
3060
.A44
1999